# The Beginner's Blueprint to Wholesaling Real Estate: Step-by-Step Coaching for Success

Clyde N. Cook, III ~ "The Real Estate Don"

# The Beginner's Blueprint to Wholesaling Real Estate: Step-by-Step Coaching for Success

The Beginner's Blueprint to Wholesaling Real Estate: Step-by-Step Coaching for Success

# The Beginner's Blueprint to Wholesaling Real Estate: Step-by-Step Coaching for Success



The Beginner's Blueprint to Wholesaling Real Estate: Step-by-Step Coaching for Success

# The Beginner's Blueprint to Wholesaling Real Estate: Step-by-Step Coaching for Success

The Beginner's Blueprint to Wholesaling Real Estate: Step-by-Step Coaching for Success

# The Beginner's Blueprint to Wholesaling Real Estate: Step-by-Step Coaching for Success

# Table Of Contents

# The Beginner's Blueprint to Wholesaling Real Estate: Step-by-Step Coaching for Success

# The Beginner's Blueprint to Wholesaling Real Estate: Step-by-Step Coaching for Success

# The Beginner's Blueprint to Wholesaling Real Estate: Step by-Step Coaching for Success

# Chapter 1: Introduction to Real Estate Wholesaling

## What is Real Estate Wholesaling?

Real estate wholesaling is a popular investment strategy that allows beginning real estate investors to enter the market with minimal risk and capital. It involves finding distressed or undervalued properties, securing them under contract, and then assigning the contract to another buyer for a profit. In essence, a real estate wholesaler acts as a middleman, connecting motivated sellers with cash buyers.

One of the key advantages of wholesaling is the low barrier to entry. Unlike other real estate investment strategies that require substantial capital or credit, wholesaling can be done with little to no money out of pocket. This makes it an attractive option for beginners who may not have a large amount of resources to invest.

To successfully wholesale a property, you need to develop a keen eye for finding distressed properties that have the potential for a profit. These properties can range from foreclosures and bank-owned homes to properties in need of significant repairs or those with motivated sellers who need to sell quickly. Finding these properties often involves networking with real estate agents, attending auctions, or conducting targeted marketing campaigns.

Once you have identified a potential deal, the next step is to negotiate a purchase agreement with the seller. This agreement should include an "assignment clause" that allows you to assign the contract to another buyer. With the contract secured, you can then market the property to potential cash buyers, such as real estate investors or rehabbers.

When you find a buyer willing to purchase the property, you can assign the contract to them for an agreed-upon fee. This fee is your profit and is typically paid at closing. The buyer then assumes the contract and completes the transaction with the original seller.

Real estate wholesaling can be a lucrative strategy for beginning investors, but it requires knowledge, persistence, and a solid network. It is important to educate yourself on local real estate laws and regulations, as well as the market conditions in your area. Building relationships with reliable contractors, real estate agents, and investors can also greatly enhance your chances of success.

In summary, real estate wholesaling is a low-risk, high-reward investment strategy that allows beginners to generate profits in the real estate market with minimal capital. By finding distressed properties, securing them under contract, and assigning the contract to another buyer, wholesalers can earn profits without the need for extensive resources or experience. With the right knowledge and networking, real estate wholesaling can be a stepping stone towards building a successful real estate investment portfolio.

## Why Choose Real Estate Wholesaling?

Real estate wholesaling is an excellent option for beginning real estate investors looking to make their mark in the industry. This subchapter will explore the various reasons why real estate wholesaling is a smart choice for those seeking success in the field.

1. Low Capital Requirements: One of the biggest advantages of real estate wholesaling is that it requires minimal upfront capital. Unlike traditional real estate investing, where substantial funds are needed to purchase properties, wholesalers act as intermediaries, connecting motivated sellers with cash buyers. This eliminates the need for large amounts of money, making it an accessible option for beginners.

2. Quick Turnaround: Real estate wholesaling offers a fast-paced business model that allows investors to earn profits within a short period. As a wholesaler, you can find distressed properties at below-market prices, negotiate favorable deals, and assign the contract to a cash buyer for a fee. This quick turnaround ensures a steady stream of income and the ability to scale your business rapidly.

3. Limited Risk: Wholesaling is a low-risk investment strategy compared to other real estate ventures. Since wholesalers don't hold onto properties, they don't need to worry about issues like property management, maintenance costs, or market fluctuations. With wholesaling, you're essentially acting as a matchmaker between buyers and sellers, reducing your exposure to potential risks.

4. No Specialized Knowledge Required: Unlike other real estate investment niches that may demand in-depth knowledge of construction, property management, or legal matters, wholesaling is relatively straightforward. While some basic understanding of the market and negotiation skills are essential, wholesaling primarily relies on networking, marketing, and negotiation abilities, making it an ideal starting point for beginners.

5. Excellent Networking Opportunities: Real estate wholesaling is a people-centric business. As a wholesaler, you'll be constantly connecting with motivated sellers, cash buyers, real estate agents, and other industry professionals. This provides ample opportunities for networking, building relationships, and expanding your business connections. These relationships can prove invaluable as you progress in your real estate journey.

In conclusion, real estate wholesaling offers a low-risk, low-capital entry point into the industry for beginning investors. Its quick turnaround, limited risk, and networking opportunities make it an attractive option for those seeking to build a successful real estate business. By choosing wholesaling as your niche, you can lay a solid foundation for future growth and profitability in the real estate market.

## The Benefits of Real Estate Wholesaling

Real estate wholesaling is a popular investment strategy that offers numerous benefits to beginning real estate investors. This subchapter will delve into the advantages of real estate wholesaling and why it is a viable option for those looking to break into the industry. Whether you are interested in real estate wholesaling coaching or simply want to understand the benefits, this section will provide you with valuable insights.

1. Minimal Capital Requirements: One of the most significant advantages of wholesaling is that it requires minimal upfront capital. Unlike other real estate investment strategies that demand substantial funds, wholesaling allows you to control properties without actually purchasing them. By acting as an intermediary between motivated sellers and cash buyers, you can earn profits through assigning contracts.

2. Quick Cash Flow: Real estate wholesaling is known for its ability to generate quick cash flow. Since the focus is on finding motivated sellers and connecting them with cash buyers, the turnaround time is relatively short. This means you can earn profits within weeks or even days, depending on the deal. For beginning investors, this can be a game-changer as it provides a steady stream of income and allows for reinvestment in future deals.

3. Low Risk: As a real estate wholesaler, you are not responsible for property ownership or long-term commitments. This significantly reduces your risk exposure compared to other real estate investment strategies. Wholesaling allows you to mitigate risks associated with market fluctuations, property management, and unexpected repairs. Since your primary role is to find and assign deals, you can avoid the pitfalls that come with property ownership.

4. Building a Network: Real estate wholesaling provides an excellent opportunity to build a strong network of industry professionals. As you engage with motivated sellers and cash buyers, you will establish relationships with real estate agents, investors, contractors, and other key players in the industry. This network can prove invaluable as you progress in your real estate career, opening doors to new opportunities, partnerships, and ongoing education.

5. Learning the Market: Wholesaling allows you to gain a deep understanding of the local real estate market. By constantly analyzing properties, negotiating deals, and assessing market trends, you will become intimately familiar with the dynamics of your target area. This knowledge can be leveraged in future ventures, enabling you to make informed investment decisions and maximize your profits.

In conclusion, real estate wholesaling offers numerous benefits to beginning real estate investors. With minimal capital requirements, quick cash flow, low risk, networking opportunities, and market insights, it is an attractive investment strategy for those looking to enter the industry. By understanding the advantages of real estate wholesaling, you can embark on a successful journey towards financial freedom and long-term real estate success.

# Common Misconceptions about Wholesaling

When it comes to real estate wholesaling, there are several common misconceptions that often mislead beginning real estate investors. Understanding these misconceptions and debunking them is crucial for anyone interested in pursuing a successful career in wholesaling. In this subchapter, we will address and clarify these misconceptions, providing you with the necessary knowledge to navigate the world of real estate wholesaling with confidence.

Misconception 1: Wholesaling is a Get-Rich-Quick Scheme
One of the biggest misconceptions about wholesaling is that it is a fast and easy way to make a fortune in real estate. The truth is that wholesaling requires hard work, dedication, and a solid understanding of the market. Success in wholesaling comes from building relationships, conducting thorough research, and consistently putting in the effort to find profitable deals.

Misconception 2: You Need a Large Amount of Money to Start Wholesaling
Contrary to popular belief, you do not need a substantial amount of capital to start wholesaling real estate. Unlike traditional real estate investing, wholesaling focuses on finding and assigning contracts, rather than purchasing properties. By leveraging your negotiation skills and building a network of buyers, you can generate income without having to invest large sums of money upfront.

Misconception 3: Wholesaling is Illegal or Unethical
Another misconception about wholesaling is that it is an illegal or unethical practice. However, when done correctly and with integrity, wholesaling is a legitimate and ethical way to make a profit in real estate. It involves helping motivated sellers find buyers for their properties and providing value to both parties involved in the transaction.

Misconception 4: Wholesaling Requires Extensive Real Estate Knowledge
While having a strong understanding of real estate can be beneficial, it is not a prerequisite for wholesaling success. Wholesaling primarily relies on effective marketing, negotiation skills, and the ability to build relationships with buyers and sellers. With proper guidance and coaching, beginning real estate investors can quickly grasp the essential concepts and techniques necessary for wholesaling.

Misconception 5: Wholesaling is a One-Time Deal
Lastly, many individuals believe that wholesaling is a one-time transaction rather than a sustainable business model. However, wholesaling can provide a consistent source of income when approached as a long-term strategy. By continuously marketing for deals, building a strong buyer's list, and staying active in the market, you can create a successful wholesaling business that generates ongoing profits.

In conclusion, understanding and dispelling common misconceptions about wholesaling is crucial for beginning real estate investors looking to succeed in the field. By debunking these myths, you can approach wholesaling with a realistic mindset and lay the foundation for a profitable and sustainable career in real estate wholesaling.

## The Wholesaling Process Overview

In the exciting world of real estate investing, wholesaling has emerged as a popular strategy among beginners due to its low entry barriers and potential for quick profits. If you're a beginning real estate investor looking to dive into the world of wholesaling, this subchapter will provide you with an essential overview of the wholesaling process.

Wholesaling real estate involves finding distressed properties at a significantly discounted price and then assigning the contract to another buyer, usually a real estate investor, for a higher price. This allows you to make a profit without actually purchasing the property yourself. The wholesaling process can be broken down into several key steps:

1. Market Research: Begin by identifying a target market and analyzing its real estate trends, demand, and supply. This will help you understand where to focus your efforts and maximize your chances of success.

2. Lead Generation: Implement various marketing strategies to generate leads, such as direct mail campaigns, online advertising, networking, and driving for dollars. The goal is to find motivated sellers who are willing to sell their distressed properties at a discount.

3. Property Evaluation: Once you've found a potential property, conduct a thorough evaluation to determine its market value, repair costs, and potential profitability. This involves assessing the property's condition, estimating repairs, and comparing it to recent sales in the area.

4. Negotiation: With a solid understanding of the property's value, negotiate with the seller to secure the property at the lowest possible price. Effective negotiation skills are crucial to ensure you can offer a competitive price to potential buyers while maintaining a healthy profit margin.

5. Contract Assignment: Once you've successfully negotiated a deal, you'll need to draft a contract that allows you to assign the rights to purchase the property to your buyer. This contract should clearly outline the terms, deadlines, and assignment fee.

6. Finding Buyers: Begin marketing the property and connecting with potential buyers, such as real estate investors, landlords, or rehabbers. Utilize both online and offline strategies to create a buzz around the property and generate interest.

7. Closing the Deal: When you've found a buyer, facilitate the closing process, ensuring that all parties are aware of the assignment and that the necessary paperwork is completed correctly. Once the deal is closed, you'll receive your assignment fee as your profit.

Understanding the wholesaling process is vital for beginning real estate investors interested in real estate wholesaling coaching. By grasping the fundamental steps involved, you can confidently navigate through each stage, increasing your chances of success. Stay tuned for the following subchapters, where we'll dive deeper into each step, providing you with invaluable insights, tips, and strategies to excel in the world of wholesaling real estate.

# Chapter 2: Getting Started in Real Estate Wholesaling

## Setting Realistic Goals

As a beginning real estate investor venturing into the world of wholesaling, it is crucial to understand the importance of setting realistic goals. Without clear objectives in mind, you may find yourself wandering aimlessly, lacking focus and direction. Setting realistic goals will not only help you stay motivated but also act as a roadmap to guide you towards success in your real estate wholesaling journey.

First and foremost, it is essential to define what success means to you. Real estate wholesaling coaching can provide you with the necessary tools and knowledge, but it is up to you to determine what you want to achieve. Are you looking to make a certain amount of profit within a specific timeframe? Do you want to build a sustainable network of buyers and sellers? Defining your goals will help you stay committed and motivated throughout the process.

Once you have a clear understanding of your goals, it is crucial to make them realistic. While it is essential to dream big, setting unattainable goals can lead to frustration and disappointment. Real estate wholesaling is a journey that requires time, effort, and dedication. Set achievable goals that challenge you but are within reach.

Another aspect to consider when setting realistic goals is to break them down into smaller, manageable milestones. By breaking your goals into smaller tasks, you can track your progress and celebrate each achievement along the way. This approach will help you stay focused and motivated, as you will be able to see tangible results.

Furthermore, it is important to set a timeline for your goals. Having a deadline will provide you with a sense of urgency and prevent procrastination. However, it is crucial to be flexible with your timeline. Real estate wholesaling is a dynamic industry, and unexpected challenges may arise. Be prepared to adjust your timeline accordingly while still maintaining a sense of urgency and progress.

Finally, it is essential to regularly review and reassess your goals. As you gain experience and knowledge in real estate wholesaling, your goals may evolve. Stay adaptable and open to change, as this will allow you to grow both personally and professionally.

In conclusion, setting realistic goals is a vital step for beginning real estate investors in the niche of real estate wholesaling coaching. By defining what success means to you, making your goals achievable and breaking them down into smaller milestones, setting a timeline, and regularly reviewing and reassessing your goals, you will be on your way to achieving success in your wholesaling journey. Stay committed, stay motivated, and remember that the path to success in real estate wholesaling starts with setting realistic goals.

## Building a Strong Mindset

In the world of real estate wholesaling, success doesn't solely depend on your knowledge of the market or your ability to negotiate deals. While these skills are undoubtedly important, what truly sets apart successful investors from the rest is their mindset. Building a strong mindset is the foundation upon which your wholesaling career can flourish.

As a beginning real estate investor, it's vital to understand that wholesaling can be a challenging and competitive industry. It requires perseverance, resilience, and a positive attitude to overcome obstacles and achieve your goals. With the right mindset, you can navigate the ups and downs of the real estate market with confidence and achieve long-term success.

One of the first steps in building a strong mindset is to establish clear goals. What do you want to achieve in your wholesaling career? Setting specific, measurable, attainable, relevant, and time-bound (SMART) goals will provide you with a roadmap to success. These goals will serve as a constant reminder of your aspirations, helping you stay focused and motivated.

Another essential aspect of building a strong mindset is cultivating a positive attitude. Real estate wholesaling can often be a rollercoaster ride, with deals falling through, negotiations failing, and setbacks occurring. However, it's crucial to maintain a positive outlook and view challenges as opportunities for growth. Embracing a "never give up" attitude will keep you motivated, even when faced with adversity.

Additionally, surrounding yourself with like-minded individuals who share your passion for real estate wholesaling can significantly impact your mindset. Seek out mentors, join real estate investment groups, and attend networking events to connect with experienced investors. Their guidance, advice, and support can help you overcome obstacles and accelerate your learning curve.

Building a strong mindset also involves continuous learning and personal development. Stay updated with industry trends, read books, listen to podcasts, and attend seminars or workshops focused on real estate wholesaling. The more knowledge and skills you acquire, the more confident and competent you will become in your wholesaling endeavors.

Lastly, don't underestimate the power of perseverance and resilience. Real estate wholesaling is a journey filled with highs and lows. It's essential to stay focused on your goals, adapt to changing circumstances, and learn from your failures. Remember, every setback is an opportunity to grow and improve.

In conclusion, building a strong mindset is crucial for beginning real estate investors in the niche of real estate wholesaling coaching. By setting clear goals, maintaining a positive attitude, surrounding yourself with supportive individuals, continuously learning, and cultivating perseverance and resilience, you can lay the foundation for a successful wholesaling career. With the right mindset, you have the power to overcome challenges, achieve your goals, and thrive in the competitive world of real estate wholesaling.

## Developing a Business Plan

As a beginning real estate investor looking to venture into the world of real estate wholesaling, it is crucial to understand the importance of developing a comprehensive business plan. A well-crafted business plan serves as a roadmap for success, allowing you to outline your goals, strategies, and tactics to achieve them. This subchapter aims to guide you through the process of creating an effective business plan specifically tailored to real estate wholesaling.

To begin, it is essential to define your overall vision and mission for your wholesaling business. What are your long-term goals? How do you want your business to be perceived in the market? Clearly articulating these aspects will help you stay focused and make informed decisions along the way.

Next, you must conduct thorough market research. Understanding your target audience, local real estate trends, and competition is crucial. This research will enable you to identify potential opportunities and develop strategies to capitalize on them.

Once you have researched the market, it's time to outline your marketing and lead generation strategies. This involves determining the channels and tactics you will employ to attract motivated sellers and build a strong network of buyers. Whether it's direct mail campaigns, online advertising, or networking events, your business plan should outline your marketing budget, schedule, and expected results.

Furthermore, you need to establish a clear plan for property acquisition and analysis. This includes identifying your criteria for selecting potential properties, conducting due diligence, and evaluating their profit potential. Your business plan should outline the key metrics and formulas you will use to determine the viability of each deal.

Financial planning is another critical aspect of your business plan. You need to establish a budget for your operations, including marketing expenses, overhead costs, and potential legal fees. Additionally, you should outline your revenue projections and cash flow analysis to ensure your business is financially sustainable.

Lastly, it is essential to develop an action plan for ongoing education and personal growth. Real estate wholesaling is a dynamic industry, and staying updated on market trends, legal regulations, and industry best practices is crucial for success. Your business plan should include a commitment to continuous learning and professional development.

In conclusion, developing a business plan is a fundamental step for beginning real estate investors interested in real estate wholesaling. It provides a roadmap to success, helps define your goals and strategies, and keeps you on track as you navigate the market. By following the guidelines outlined in this subchapter, you will be well-prepared to embark on your wholesaling journey and achieve your financial goals.

## Understanding Market Analysis

Market analysis is a crucial aspect of real estate wholesaling. As a beginning real estate investor, it is essential to grasp the concept of market analysis to make informed decisions and achieve success in the highly competitive world of real estate wholesaling.

Market analysis involves evaluating the current state of the real estate market, including supply and demand, pricing trends, and market conditions. By understanding the market dynamics, you can identify profitable opportunities and avoid potential pitfalls.

One key factor of market analysis is understanding supply and demand. A market with high demand and limited supply creates a favorable environment for real estate wholesalers. You can identify such markets by analyzing factors such as population growth, job opportunities, and economic indicators. Additionally, studying the inventory of available properties and the average time they spend on the market can provide valuable insights into supply and demand dynamics.

Pricing trends are another crucial aspect of market analysis. Analyzing the recent sales data of comparable properties in a specific area can help you determine the fair market value of a property. This information is vital for negotiating favorable deals and ensuring that you can sell the property for a profit.

Market conditions also play a significant role in real estate wholesaling. Factors such as interest rates, government policies, and local regulations can impact the real estate market. Staying informed about these conditions can help you anticipate market trends and adapt your strategies accordingly.

To conduct a comprehensive market analysis, it is essential to gather data from various sources, including real estate websites, local government reports, and industry publications. Additionally, networking with experienced real estate professionals and attending industry events can provide valuable insights and help you stay up-to-date with market trends.

By understanding market analysis, beginning real estate investors can make informed decisions and increase their chances of success in real estate wholesaling. Comprehensive market analysis allows you to identify lucrative opportunities, negotiate favorable deals, and adapt your strategies to changing market conditions. As you gain experience and refine your market analysis skills, you will be better equipped to navigate the complexities of the real estate market and achieve your wholesaling goals.

## Building Your Network of Professionals

As a beginning real estate investor, one of the most crucial steps you can take towards success in the world of real estate wholesaling is building a strong network of professionals. These professionals will be your support system, guiding you through the intricacies of the industry and providing valuable insights and advice along the way. In this subchapter, we will explore the key individuals you should connect with to enhance your real estate wholesaling journey.

1. Real Estate Agents: Real estate agents are an invaluable resource for beginner investors. They possess extensive knowledge of the local market, understand property valuations, and have access to a wide range of listings. Establishing relationships with reputable agents can help you find lucrative wholesale deals and gain access to off-market properties.

2. Contractors: Developing a network of reliable and skilled contractors is essential for successful real estate wholesaling. These professionals can help you accurately estimate repair costs, execute necessary renovations, and improve the overall value of a property. By collaborating with contractors, you can ensure your deals are profitable and completed efficiently.

3. Attorneys: Legal matters are an integral part of any real estate transaction. Having a competent attorney in your network will protect you from potential legal pitfalls and ensure all contracts and agreements are properly drafted and executed. Attorneys specialized in real estate can guide you through the legal intricacies of wholesale deals, ensuring compliance with local regulations.

4. Title Companies: Title companies play a vital role in real estate transactions by conducting title searches, issuing title insurance, and handling the closing process. Building relationships with reputable title companies will streamline your wholesale deals and provide you with peace of mind regarding the property's ownership and any potential liens or encumbrances.

5. Investors and Mentors: Connecting with seasoned real estate investors and mentors can provide you with invaluable guidance and support. These individuals have already navigated the challenges and pitfalls of real estate wholesaling and can offer insights into market trends, negotiation strategies, and deal structuring.

6. Mortgage Brokers: Mortgage brokers can assist you in securing financing for your wholesale deals. By establishing relationships with brokers, you can access a variety of loan products and favorable terms, enhancing your ability to close deals quickly.

Remember, building a network of professionals takes time and effort. Attend local real estate investor meetups, join online forums, and actively seek out opportunities to connect with individuals in the industry. Nurture these relationships by offering value, staying engaged, and being a reliable resource yourself. By building a strong network of professionals, you'll gain access to invaluable resources, expand your knowledge base, and increase your chances of success in the world of real estate wholesaling.

# Chapter 3: Finding Lucrative Wholesaling Deals

## Identifying Distressed Properties

Identifying Distressed Properties: Uncovering Hidden Opportunities in Real Estate Wholesaling

As a beginning real estate investor venturing into the world of real estate wholesaling, one of the most crucial skills you must develop is the ability to identify distressed properties. These properties present a golden opportunity for you to secure lucrative deals and make a substantial profit. In this subchapter, we will explore the key strategies and techniques that will help you identify distressed properties and unlock their hidden potential.

Distressed properties, also known as fixer-uppers or distressed homes, are properties that are in a state of disrepair or facing financial difficulties. These properties often require significant repairs, have motivated sellers, or are in foreclosure. By targeting distressed properties, you can negotiate favorable purchase terms and acquire properties below market value, setting the stage for profitable wholesaling transactions.

One effective way to identify distressed properties is through targeted marketing campaigns. By leveraging online platforms, social media, and direct mail, you can reach out to homeowners facing financial challenges or those who own properties in need of repairs. Offering solutions and highlighting the benefits of a quick sale can attract motivated sellers to reach out to you.

Another approach is to establish relationships with local real estate agents and brokers who specialize in distressed properties. These professionals have access to databases and networks that can provide you with a steady stream of potential deals. Networking and attending industry events can also open doors to off-market distressed properties.

In addition, staying updated with public records, such as foreclosure listings or tax delinquencies, can be a valuable source of distressed property leads. Many municipalities make this information available online, allowing you to identify properties that are at risk of foreclosure or have fallen behind on property taxes.

Furthermore, driving for dollars – physically scouting neighborhoods in your target area – can be an effective strategy. Look for signs of neglect, such as boarded-up windows, overgrown lawns, or mail piling up. These visual cues often indicate owners who may be motivated to sell their distressed property.

By honing your skills in identifying distressed properties, you will be able to uncover hidden opportunities and establish a strong foundation for your real estate wholesaling business. Remember, diligence, creativity, and persistence are key in this endeavor. Stay tuned for the following subchapters where we will delve into the art of negotiating with motivated sellers and structuring profitable deals. Happy wholesaling!

## Analyzing Potential Deals

One of the key skills that every beginning real estate investor needs to develop is the ability to analyze potential deals. This is especially true for those interested in real estate wholesaling, as finding and securing profitable properties is the foundation of this investment strategy. In this subchapter, we will explore the essential steps and techniques involved in analyzing potential deals, helping you make informed decisions and maximize your success as a real estate wholesaling investor.

The first step in analyzing potential deals is to establish your investment criteria. This means identifying the specific types of properties you are interested in, such as single-family homes, multi-unit buildings, or commercial properties. Additionally, you should determine your target market, taking into account factors such as location, property value, and potential for appreciation. By defining your investment criteria, you can focus your efforts on finding deals that align with your goals and preferences.

Next, you need to learn how to evaluate the financial aspects of a potential deal. This includes conducting a thorough analysis of the property's value, potential repairs or renovations needed, and estimated rental or resale income. You should familiarize yourself with key financial indicators such as the net operating income (NOI), cash-on-cash return, and return on investment (ROI). By understanding these metrics, you can accurately assess the profitability of a potential deal and determine whether it meets your investment criteria.

Furthermore, it is crucial to conduct a comprehensive market analysis. This involves researching and understanding the local real estate market, including supply and demand dynamics, property values, rental rates, and market trends. By staying informed about the market conditions, you can make more informed decisions and identify potential opportunities or risks.

To aid in your deal analysis, you should also leverage technology and real estate wholesaling coaching resources. There are various online tools and software available that can help automate and streamline the deal analysis process. Additionally, seeking guidance from experienced real estate wholesaling coaches or mentors can provide invaluable insights and strategies for analyzing potential deals effectively.

In conclusion, analyzing potential deals is a critical skill for beginning real estate investors, especially those interested in real estate wholesaling. By establishing your investment criteria, evaluating the financial aspects, conducting market analysis, and leveraging technology and coaching resources, you can make informed decisions and increase your chances of securing profitable deals. Remember, thorough analysis and due diligence are essential for success in the real estate wholesaling business.

## Marketing Strategies for Finding Deals

One of the most crucial aspects of successful real estate wholesaling is finding lucrative deals. As a beginning real estate investor, understanding and implementing effective marketing strategies can make all the difference in your success. In this subchapter, we will explore various marketing strategies specifically tailored for finding deals, ensuring that you have a solid foundation for your wholesaling business.

1. Direct Mail Campaigns: Direct mail is a tried and tested method for reaching potential sellers. Craft well-written letters and postcards that highlight the benefits of selling their property to you. Target specific demographics or distressed property owners to maximize your chances of finding motivated sellers.

2. Bandit Signs: Placing eye-catching bandit signs in strategic locations can generate leads. These signs should include your contact information and a simple message such as "We Buy Houses for Cash." Be mindful of local regulations and always seek permission before placing signs.

3. Online Marketing: Establishing an online presence is crucial in today's digital age. Create a professional website and optimize it for search engines. Utilize social media platforms, such as Facebook and Instagram, to reach a wider audience. Consider running targeted online ads to attract motivated sellers and investors.

4. Networking: Building a strong network within the real estate industry is invaluable. Attend local real estate meetups, join investor clubs, and connect with other professionals in the field. Networking can lead to potential partnerships, referrals, and access to off-market deals.

5. Referrals: Encourage referrals from friends, family, and colleagues. Offer incentives, such as a finders fee, for any deals that close as a result of their referrals. Word-of-mouth marketing can be incredibly powerful in finding motivated sellers.

6. Cold Calling: Although it may seem daunting, cold calling can be an effective way to find deals. Create a script and practice it to ensure confident and professional communication. Target motivated sellers or distressed property owners and be prepared to handle objections.

7. Driving for Dollars: Get out and explore neighborhoods in search of distressed or vacant properties. Take note of any potential leads and reach out to the owners. This hands-on approach can uncover hidden gems that others may overlook.

Remember, consistency is key when implementing marketing strategies. Create a comprehensive marketing plan and allocate time and resources to execute it consistently. Monitor your efforts, track results, and adjust your strategies accordingly to optimize your success.

By implementing these marketing strategies for finding deals, you will position yourself as a knowledgeable and motivated wholesaler in the real estate industry. With time and dedication, you will build a robust pipeline of deals that will contribute to your success as a beginning real estate investor.

## Negotiating with Sellers

Subchapter: Negotiating with Sellers

Introduction:
Negotiating with sellers is a crucial skill that every beginning real estate investor must master. It is during these negotiations that you will be able to secure favorable deals and maximize your profits. In this subchapter, we will explore effective strategies and techniques that will help you become a skilled negotiator in the world of real estate wholesaling.

Understanding the Seller's Motivation:
Before diving into negotiations, it is essential to understand the seller's motivation. Are they in a hurry to sell? Are they facing financial difficulties or foreclosure? Knowing their underlying reasons will give you an advantage in structuring a deal that meets their needs while also benefiting you. Take the time to listen and empathize with their situation, as this will help you build a rapport and establish a foundation for negotiation.

Setting the Stage:
When negotiating with sellers, it is important to set the stage for a successful outcome. Arrive prepared with a comprehensive market analysis, comparable sales data, and any other relevant information that supports your offer. Present yourself as a knowledgeable and trustworthy investor who can provide a quick and hassle-free solution to their problem.

Creating Win-Win Scenarios:
Negotiations should always aim to create win-win scenarios where both parties benefit. Seek to understand the seller's desired outcome and find creative ways to meet their needs while still leaving room for profitability on your end. Offer multiple options and strive for flexibility in your approach. By demonstrating empathy and actively listening to their concerns, you can craft a deal that works for everyone involved.

Mastering the Art of Persuasion:
Effective negotiation requires mastering the art of persuasion. Learn to communicate your value proposition clearly and confidently. Highlight the benefits of working with you as a wholesaler, such as a quick closing, cash offers, and taking care of all the necessary paperwork. Use your knowledge of the market and industry to convince sellers that your offer is fair and in their best interest.

Overcoming Objections:
During negotiations, sellers may voice objections or concerns. It is crucial to address these objections calmly and professionally. Anticipate common objections and come prepared with well-thought-out responses. By acknowledging and addressing their concerns, you can build trust and increase the likelihood of reaching a favorable agreement.

Closing the Deal:
Once negotiations reach a mutually agreeable point, it's time to close the deal. Ensure that all terms and conditions are clearly spelled out in a written agreement, and consult with legal professionals if necessary. Maintain open lines of communication with the seller throughout the closing process, providing updates and addressing any concerns promptly.

Conclusion:
Negotiating with sellers is an essential skill for any beginning real estate investor looking to succeed in the world of wholesaling. By understanding the seller's motivations, setting the stage, creating win-win scenarios, mastering persuasion, overcoming objections, and closing the deal, you can establish yourself as a successful wholesaler who consistently secures profitable opportunities. With practice and experience, your negotiation skills will continue to improve, allowing you to maximize your profits and build a successful real estate wholesaling business.

# Due Diligence and Property Inspections

Due Diligence and Property Inspections: The Cornerstones of Successful Wholesaling

As a beginning real estate investor, you may have heard the term "due diligence" thrown around quite a bit. But what exactly does it mean, and why is it crucial for your success in the world of real estate wholesaling? In this subchapter, we will delve into the importance of due diligence and property inspections and explore how they can make or break your deals.

Due diligence refers to the process of thoroughly researching and investigating a property before making a purchase. It involves gathering relevant information, analyzing the property's value, and assessing its potential risks and opportunities. By conducting due diligence, you can ensure that you are making informed decisions and avoid costly surprises down the road.

One of the key aspects of due diligence is conducting property inspections. These inspections provide you with a comprehensive understanding of the property's condition, identifying any potential issues that may affect its value or marketability. A thorough inspection can uncover hidden structural problems, plumbing or electrical issues, or even environmental hazards that may not be immediately apparent.

To conduct a proper property inspection, it is crucial to hire a qualified and experienced professional. A licensed home inspector can assess the property's overall condition, including its foundation, roof, HVAC systems, and more. It is also advisable to consult other specialists, such as plumbers, electricians, or pest control experts, depending on the specific needs of the property.

During the inspection, take the time to accompany the inspector and ask questions. This will not only help you gain valuable knowledge about the property but also demonstrate your commitment to thorough due diligence to potential buyers or sellers.

Remember, due diligence and property inspections are not just about avoiding pitfalls but also about uncovering opportunities. By thoroughly understanding a property's strengths and weaknesses, you can negotiate better deals, estimate repair costs accurately, and market the property effectively.

In conclusion, due diligence and property inspections are the cornerstones of successful wholesaling. By investing time and effort into these crucial steps, beginning real estate investors can minimize risks, maximize profits, and build a reputation for professionalism within the real estate wholesaling coaching niche. So, embrace due diligence, conduct thorough property inspections, and pave the way for your success in the exciting world of real estate wholesaling.

# Chapter 4: Building a Reliable Buyer's List

## Identifying Your Target Buyers

One of the key aspects of successful real estate wholesaling is understanding and identifying your target buyers. As a beginning real estate investor, it is crucial to have a clear understanding of who your potential buyers are in order to maximize your profits and minimize risks. In this subchapter, we will delve into the process of identifying your target buyers and provide you with valuable insights and strategies to ensure your wholesaling business thrives.

The first step in identifying your target buyers is to conduct thorough market research. Understanding your local market trends and demographics will help you identify the type of properties that are in demand and the ideal buyers for those properties. Analyze factors such as average income levels, employment rates, and population growth to gain a comprehensive understanding of your target market.

Next, consider the specific niches within the real estate wholesaling coaching industry. Are you targeting first-time homebuyers, real estate investors, or rehabbers? Each niche has its own unique needs and preferences, and tailoring your wholesaling business to cater to these niches can greatly increase your chances of success. For example, if you are targeting rehabbers, you should focus on finding distressed properties that require significant renovation work.

Once you have identified your target market and niche, it is important to develop a buyer persona. A buyer persona is a detailed profile of your ideal buyer, including their demographics, preferences, and motivations. This will help you tailor your marketing and acquisition strategies to attract the right buyers.

In addition to understanding your target buyers, it is also crucial to build and maintain relationships with potential buyers in your market. Attend local real estate networking events, join online forums, and reach out to other real estate professionals to expand your network. Building a strong buyer's list will give you a competitive advantage and increase your chances of finding qualified buyers for your wholesale deals.

Lastly, continuously evaluate and refine your marketing strategies to ensure they are effective in reaching your target buyers. Monitor and track the performance of your marketing campaigns, and make adjustments as needed. Stay up-to-date with the latest marketing trends and techniques to stay ahead of the competition and maximize your chances of success.

By identifying your target buyers and tailoring your wholesaling business to meet their needs, you can position yourself as a trusted and valuable resource in the real estate market. With a clear understanding of your target buyers, a strong buyer's list, and effective marketing strategies, you will be well on your way to achieving wholesaling success.

## Marketing Your Wholesale Deals

As a beginning real estate investor in the niche of real estate wholesaling, it is essential to understand the importance of effectively marketing your wholesale deals. Marketing is the key to attracting potential buyers and securing profitable deals. In this subchapter, we will discuss various strategies and techniques to market your wholesale deals successfully.

1. Develop a Strong Online Presence:
In today's digital age, having a strong online presence is crucial. Create a professional website to showcase your wholesale deals, including detailed property descriptions, high-quality images, and contact information. Utilize social media platforms such as Facebook, Instagram, and LinkedIn to reach a wider audience and engage with potential buyers.

**2. Build Relationships with Investors:**
Networking and building relationships with other real estate investors is a powerful marketing tool. Attend local real estate investment meetings, join online forums, and participate in industry events to connect with potential buyers. Establishing a strong network will not only help you find buyers for your wholesale deals but also provide valuable insights and opportunities for collaboration.

**3. Utilize Direct Mail Campaigns:**
Direct mail campaigns can be an effective way to target potential buyers. Create engaging and personalized mailers highlighting the benefits and potential profits of your wholesale deals. Include your contact information, website, and a call-to-action to encourage recipients to reach out to you for more information.

**4. Leverage Online Listing Platforms:**
Listing your wholesale deals on online platforms dedicated to real estate investments, such as BiggerPockets or LoopNet, can significantly increase your reach. These platforms attract a vast audience of real estate investors actively searching for lucrative deals. Ensure your listings are complete, accurate, and compelling to capture potential buyers' attention.

5. Develop a Strong Brand:
Creating a strong brand will help you stand out from the competition and establish credibility in the market. Develop a memorable logo, tagline, and brand identity that resonates with your target audience. Consistently incorporate your brand elements into your marketing materials, website, and social media platforms to create a cohesive and professional image.

6. Collaborate with Local Real Estate Agents:
Real estate agents often have a vast network of potential buyers. Collaborating with them can be mutually beneficial. Offer incentives to agents who bring buyers for your wholesale deals, such as a percentage of the profits or exclusive access to future opportunities.

Remember, effective marketing is an ongoing process. Continuously evaluate and refine your strategies based on the feedback and results you receive. By implementing these marketing techniques, you will increase your chances of finding qualified buyers and achieving success in your real estate wholesaling journey.

# Creating an Effective Buyer's List

One of the key factors in achieving success as a beginning real estate investor, particularly in the realm of real estate wholesaling, is building a strong and effective buyer's list. A buyer's list consists of individuals or companies interested in purchasing wholesale properties for investment purposes. This subchapter will guide you through the process of creating an effective buyer's list, providing you with step-by-step instructions and essential tips to ensure your success in real estate wholesaling.

The first step in creating a buyer's list is identifying your target audience. Determine the niches within the real estate market that you want to focus on, such as rental property investors, fix-and-flip enthusiasts, or commercial property buyers. By understanding your target audience, you can tailor your marketing efforts and attract the right buyers for your properties.

Next, you need to employ various marketing strategies to build your buyer's list. Utilize both online and offline channels to reach potential buyers. Online platforms like social media, real estate forums, and local listing websites can help you connect with interested investors. Offline strategies may include attending real estate networking events, joining local real estate investment associations, and distributing flyers or business cards at industry-related gatherings.

To attract buyers, it's crucial to showcase the value you bring as a wholesaler. Highlight your knowledge of the local market, your ability to secure profitable deals, and your commitment to providing exceptional customer service. Offer incentives such as exclusive access to off-market properties or preferential pricing for repeat buyers. These perks will motivate investors to join your buyer's list and increase your credibility within the industry.

Regularly communicate with the individuals on your buyer's list to nurture relationships and keep them engaged. Send out newsletters or emails with updates on new properties, market trends, and investment opportunities. Providing valuable content will position you as a trusted resource and keep your list active and responsive.

Remember, building an effective buyer's list is an ongoing process. Continuously seek out new investors, update your list with fresh contacts, and refine your strategies based on market changes and feedback from buyers. As you gain experience and expand your network, your buyer's list will become a valuable asset in your real estate wholesaling business.

By following the steps outlined in this subchapter and consistently implementing effective marketing strategies, you will create a robust and successful buyer's list that will propel your career as a real estate wholesaler.

# Networking with Investors

# The Beginner's Blueprint to Wholesaling Real Estate: Step-by-Step Coaching for Success

As a beginning real estate investor, one of the most valuable skills you can develop is networking with investors. Building relationships with fellow investors can open up a world of opportunities and help you accelerate your success in the real estate wholesaling industry. In this chapter, we will explore the importance of networking, the benefits it offers, and practical tips to help you network effectively.

Why is networking important in real estate wholesaling? Well, investing in real estate is not a solitary endeavor. It requires a network of professionals, including investors, real estate agents, contractors, and more, to navigate the complexities of the market successfully. By networking with investors, you gain access to their knowledge, experiences, and resources. They can offer guidance, share insights, and provide opportunities for collaboration or partnership.

The benefits of networking with investors are numerous. Firstly, it allows you to tap into a wealth of knowledge and expertise. Experienced investors have likely encountered various challenges and can offer valuable advice on how to overcome them. They can also share strategies and best practices that have worked for them in the past.

Secondly, networking enables you to expand your circle of influence. By connecting with successful investors, you gain exposure to a wider audience and can leverage their reputation and credibility. This can open doors to potential deals, partnerships, and funding opportunities that may not have been accessible otherwise.

To network effectively with investors, it is essential to adopt a proactive approach. Attend local real estate investment clubs, seminars, and conferences where investors gather. These events provide an excellent opportunity to meet like-minded individuals, exchange ideas, and establish relationships. Additionally, utilize online platforms such as LinkedIn or real estate forums to connect with investors from different regions or niches.

When networking, remember that it is a two-way street. Be genuinely interested in others and their businesses. Listen attentively and ask insightful questions. Offer your expertise or assistance whenever possible. Building a strong network is about fostering mutually beneficial relationships, not just seeking opportunities for yourself.

Lastly, don't underestimate the power of networking within your own niche. Seek out real estate wholesaling coaching programs or mentorship opportunities where you can connect with experienced wholesalers. They can provide valuable insights into the specific challenges and strategies related to wholesaling.

In conclusion, networking with investors is crucial for beginning real estate investors in the niche of real estate wholesaling coaching. It offers a gateway to knowledge, resources, and opportunities that can fast-track your success. By actively participating in networking events, engaging with fellow investors, and building meaningful relationships, you can create a strong network that will support your growth and help you achieve your wholesaling goals.

## Maintaining and Growing Your Buyer's List

One of the most crucial aspects of being a successful real estate wholesaler is having a strong and constantly growing buyer's list. Your buyer's list consists of individuals or companies who are interested in purchasing properties from you at a discounted price. These buyers are essential to your business as they provide the necessary liquidity for your deals and ensure a quick turnaround.

As a beginning real estate investor, it is vital to understand the importance of maintaining and growing your buyer's list. In this subchapter, we will explore the strategies and techniques that will help you build a strong buyer's list and keep it thriving.

First and foremost, networking is the key to maintaining and growing your buyer's list. Attend real estate investor meetups, join online forums and groups, and actively participate in industry events. Building relationships with other investors and professionals in the field will not only expand your knowledge but also expose you to potential buyers.

Utilizing online platforms is another effective way to grow your buyer's list. Create a website or landing page where interested buyers can sign up to receive alerts and updates about your latest properties. Use social media platforms like Facebook and LinkedIn to connect with potential buyers and share valuable content related to real estate investing.

Furthermore, always prioritize communication with your existing buyers. Regularly reach out to them with updates on new properties, market trends, and investment opportunities. Building trust and maintaining open lines of communication will solidify your relationship and increase the chances of repeat business.

Consider offering incentives to your buyers as a way to grow your list. Provide exclusive access to off-market deals or offer special discounts for repeat buyers. By offering added value, you can attract more potential buyers and keep them engaged in your offerings.

Finally, leverage partnerships and collaborations with other real estate professionals to expand your buyer's list. Build relationships with real estate agents, property management companies, and other wholesalers. By working together, you can cross-promote each other's properties and tap into each other's buyer networks.

In conclusion, maintaining and growing your buyer's list is crucial for success in real estate wholesaling. Networking, online platforms, communication, incentives, and strategic partnerships are all valuable tools to help you achieve this goal. By implementing these strategies and continuously nurturing your buyer relationships, you will establish a strong foundation for your wholesaling business and pave the way for long-term success as a beginning real estate investor.

# Chapter 5: Contracting and Assigning Wholesale Deals

## Understanding Purchase Agreements

In the world of real estate wholesaling, one of the most crucial documents you need to familiarize yourself with is the purchase agreement. This legal contract serves as the foundation of any real estate transaction and outlines the terms and conditions agreed upon between the buyer and the seller. As a beginning real estate investor, it is essential to understand the ins and outs of purchase agreements to navigate the wholesaling process successfully.

A purchase agreement is a binding contract that outlines the details of the property being sold, the purchase price, and any contingencies or conditions that must be met before the deal can be finalized. It is crucial to have a well-drafted purchase agreement to protect your interests and ensure a smooth transaction.

When drafting or reviewing a purchase agreement, pay close attention to the following key elements:

1. Purchase Price: Clearly state the agreed-upon purchase price for the property. This includes any additional costs or fees associated with the transaction.

2. Property Description: Provide a detailed description of the property, including the address, legal description, and any specific features or conditions that may affect its value.

3. Contingencies: Include any contingencies or conditions that must be met before the purchase can be completed. Common contingencies include inspection periods, financing arrangements, or the sale of another property.

4. Earnest Money: Specify the amount of earnest money (a deposit made by the buyer to show good faith) and the deadline for its submission. This demonstrates your commitment to the deal and provides compensation to the seller if you fail to fulfill your obligations.

5. Closing Date: Clearly state the closing date, which is the deadline for completing the transaction. This allows all parties involved to plan accordingly and ensures a timely process.

6. Disclosures: Include any necessary disclosures required by law, such as known defects, lead-based paint, or other potential issues that could impact the buyer's decision.

Remember, a purchase agreement is a legally binding contract, so it is crucial to have an attorney review or assist you in creating one. This will ensure that your interests are protected and that all necessary legal requirements are met.

Understanding purchase agreements is vital for any beginning real estate investor looking to succeed in the world of real estate wholesaling. By grasping the key elements and seeking professional advice when necessary, you can confidently navigate the intricacies of purchase agreements and secure profitable deals in the competitive real estate market.

## Writing Effective Contracts

When it comes to real estate wholesaling, one of the most important aspects of your business is the contracts you use. Contracts are the backbone of any real estate transaction, and understanding how to draft and negotiate them effectively is crucial for success as a beginning real estate investor.

The purpose of a contract is to outline the terms and conditions of the agreement between the buyer and the seller. It serves as a legally binding document that protects both parties and ensures that everyone involved understands their rights and obligations. As a real estate wholesaler, it is essential to have a solid understanding of contract law and how to create effective contracts that protect your interests.

The first step in writing an effective contract is to clearly define the terms of the agreement. This includes specifying the purchase price, the property address, and any contingencies or conditions that must be met before the contract can be executed. It's important to be as detailed as possible to avoid any potential misunderstandings or disputes down the line.

Additionally, it's crucial to include provisions that protect your interests as a wholesaler. This may include an assignment clause, which allows you to assign the contract to another buyer without obtaining the seller's consent. This flexibility is one of the key advantages of wholesaling real estate, and having a well-drafted assignment clause can make your business more efficient and profitable.

Furthermore, it's essential to include clauses that address potential risks and liabilities. For example, a due diligence clause allows you to inspect the property and verify its condition before moving forward with the transaction. This protects you from unexpected repairs or issues that may arise after the contract is signed.

Finally, it's important to consult with a qualified attorney or real estate professional when drafting your contracts. They can provide valuable guidance and ensure that your contracts comply with local laws and regulations. Investing in the expertise of professionals can save you time, money, and potential legal troubles in the long run.

In conclusion, writing effective contracts is a vital skill for beginning real estate investors in the niche of real estate wholesaling coaching. By clearly defining the terms of the agreement, including provisions that protect your interests, and consulting with professionals, you can ensure that your contracts are legally sound and set the foundation for successful wholesaling transactions.

## Assignment of Contracts

One fundamental aspect of real estate wholesaling that every beginning real estate investor should understand is the assignment of contracts. This subchapter will delve into the concept of assigning contracts and explain how it is an essential tool for success in the real estate wholesaling business.

When it comes to wholesaling real estate, assigning contracts allows investors to profit from a deal without actually purchasing the property. This strategy is particularly attractive for those who have limited funds or want to minimize the risks associated with owning properties. By assigning contracts, investors can essentially act as intermediaries between motivated sellers and cash buyers, facilitating a mutually beneficial transaction.

The assignment of contracts involves three key parties: the wholesaler (assignor), the seller, and the buyer (assignee). The wholesaler initially finds a distressed property with potential for profit and negotiates a purchase agreement with the seller. This agreement establishes the price and terms of the deal. However, instead of closing on the property themselves, the wholesaler assigns their rights and obligations under the contract to the buyer, who then steps in and completes the transaction.

To effectively assign contracts, beginning real estate investors must understand the following steps:

1. Identify potential wholesale deals: Develop a comprehensive understanding of the market and criteria for identifying distressed properties with profit potential.

2. Negotiate purchase agreements: Learn effective negotiation techniques to secure favorable terms with motivated sellers.

3. Draft assignment agreements: Create legally binding contracts that clearly outline the assignment of rights and obligations to the buyer.

4. Market the contract for assignment: Utilize various marketing strategies and networks to find cash buyers interested in purchasing the contract.

5. Coordinate the transaction: Facilitate communication between the seller, buyer, and any other relevant parties to ensure a smooth and successful closing.

By mastering the art of assigning contracts, beginning real estate investors can generate income without the need for substantial capital or credit. However, it is crucial to conduct thorough due diligence, understand local laws and regulations, and seek legal advice to ensure compliance and mitigate potential risks.

In conclusion, the assignment of contracts is a powerful tool that allows beginning real estate investors to profit from wholesaling properties without actually owning them. By understanding and implementing the steps outlined in this subchapter, aspiring real estate wholesalers can lay the foundation for a successful and lucrative career in the industry.

## Closing the Deal

Closing the deal is the most crucial part of the real estate wholesaling process. It is the moment that all your hard work and negotiations come to fruition. In this subchapter, we will explore the essential steps to successfully close a deal and provide you with the tools and strategies to make it happen.

1. Prepare for Closing: Before the closing date, it is essential to gather all the necessary documents and paperwork. This includes the purchase agreement, assignment contract, and any other relevant documents. Ensure that all parties involved have signed the necessary paperwork and that you have a clear understanding of the terms and conditions of the deal.

2. Secure Financing: If you have secured a buyer for the property, make sure they have the necessary financing in place to close the deal. Communicate with your buyer and their lender to ensure all the financial aspects are in order. If necessary, provide any additional documentation or information required by the lender to facilitate a smooth closing process.

3. Conduct Due Diligence: As the closing date approaches, conduct a final walkthrough of the property to ensure it is in the condition agreed upon. Address any last-minute repairs or issues that may have arisen since the initial inspection. It is crucial to maintain open lines of communication with both the buyer and the seller to ensure everyone is on the same page.

4. Schedule the Closing: Work with a trusted title company or attorney to schedule the closing. Ensure that all parties involved are available on the designated date and time. Double-check that all required documents will be prepared and available for review and signing.

5. Attend the Closing: On the day of closing, be present and prepared. Bring all necessary documents and identification to the closing table. Review each document carefully before signing and ask any questions you may have. Ensure that all terms and conditions of the deal are accurately reflected in the closing documents.

6. Collect Your Assignment Fee: Once the deal has successfully closed, it is time to collect your assignment fee. This is the profit you have negotiated as the wholesaler. Coordinate with the closing agent to ensure the fee is disbursed correctly and in a timely manner.

Closing the deal can be both exciting and nerve-wracking for beginning real estate investors. However, by following these essential steps and maintaining open lines of communication throughout the process, you can ensure a successful closing. Remember, thorough preparation and attention to detail are key to closing deals effectively in the real estate wholesaling business.

In the next subchapter, we will explore strategies for evaluating potential properties and identifying profitable deals. Stay tuned for more valuable insights and guidance on your journey to becoming a successful real estate wholesaler.

## Avoiding Common Legal Pitfalls

One of the most crucial aspects of becoming a successful real estate wholesaler is understanding and navigating the legal landscape. As a beginning real estate investor, it is imperative to be aware of the common legal pitfalls that can arise in this industry. By familiarizing yourself with these potential challenges and adopting proactive strategies to mitigate them, you can ensure a smooth and profitable journey in real estate wholesaling.

One of the first legal aspects to consider is ensuring compliance with local laws and regulations. Real estate laws can vary significantly from one jurisdiction to another, and it is essential to understand the specific rules and requirements in your area. Failure to comply with these regulations can lead to severe consequences, including fines, legal disputes, or even the suspension of your wholesaling activities. Therefore, it is crucial to consult with a local attorney or real estate professional to gain a comprehensive understanding of the legal framework in your region.

Another common legal pitfall in real estate wholesaling is the improper use of contracts. Contracts serve as the foundation for any real estate transaction, and it is essential to ensure that they are legally binding and accurately reflect the agreed-upon terms. Mistakes or omissions in contracts can lead to disputes, delays, or even the collapse of a deal. To avoid this, consider working with an experienced real estate attorney who can help you draft and review contracts to protect your interests.

Additionally, understanding fair housing laws is essential to avoid legal troubles. Discrimination in real estate is strictly prohibited, and it is crucial to treat all potential sellers and buyers fairly and equally. Familiarize yourself with federal, state, and local fair housing laws to ensure you are not inadvertently violating any regulations. Discriminatory practices can lead to lawsuits, damaged reputation, and financial penalties.

Lastly, it is important to consider the potential legal implications of marketing strategies used in real estate wholesaling. Some marketing techniques, such as direct mail campaigns or cold calling, may be subject to specific regulations, such as the Do Not Call Registry. Failing to adhere to these regulations can result in legal consequences and damage your reputation as a wholesaler. Ensure that your marketing efforts comply with all applicable laws and regulations to avoid potential legal pitfalls.

In conclusion, as a beginning real estate investor, it is vital to be aware of the common legal pitfalls in real estate wholesaling. By understanding and proactively addressing these potential challenges, you can navigate the legal landscape with confidence and protect yourself from legal troubles. Remember to consult with local professionals, use proper contracts, comply with fair housing laws, and adhere to marketing regulations. By doing so, you will set yourself up for success in your real estate wholesaling journey.

# Chapter 6: Marketing and Advertising Strategies for Wholesalers

## Creating a Personal Brand

In the world of real estate investing, building a personal brand can be the key to your success. As a beginning real estate investor, it is crucial to understand the importance of establishing a strong personal brand that sets you apart from your competitors. This subchapter will guide you through the process of creating a unique personal brand that resonates with your target audience.

To begin, it is important to understand what a personal brand entails. Your personal brand is a reflection of who you are, what you stand for, and what you bring to the table as a real estate wholesaler. It is the image and reputation you portray in the industry. By creating a personal brand, you are establishing yourself as an expert and building trust with potential clients.

The first step in creating a personal brand is defining your niche. Real estate wholesaling coaching is a competitive field, so finding a specific niche will help you stand out. Consider your strengths, interests, and expertise to determine your niche. Are you particularly skilled at finding off-market properties or negotiating deals? Identifying your niche will allow you to focus your efforts and attract clients who are specifically seeking your expertise.

Once you have identified your niche, it is time to develop your brand identity. This includes your logo, color palette, and overall visual aesthetic. Your brand identity should align with your niche and target audience. For example, if your niche is luxury properties, your brand identity should reflect sophistication and elegance. Consistency is key in branding, so ensure that your brand identity is reflected across all your marketing materials, including your website, social media profiles, and business cards.

In addition to visual branding, it is essential to create a strong online presence. Utilize social media platforms such as Facebook, Instagram, and LinkedIn to showcase your expertise and build credibility. Share valuable content, engage with your audience, and establish yourself as a thought leader in the industry. A professional website is also crucial for building your personal brand. Ensure that your website is user-friendly, visually appealing, and showcases your success stories and testimonials.

Lastly, building a personal brand requires consistency and persistence. Continuously refine your brand messaging and adapt to industry trends. Stay active in networking events, attend real estate conferences, and engage with other professionals in the field. By consistently building your personal brand, you will attract more clients, establish yourself as a trusted expert, and ultimately achieve success in real estate wholesaling coaching.

Remember, creating a personal brand takes time and effort, but the rewards are worth it. By following the steps outlined in this subchapter, you will be well on your way to building a strong personal brand that sets you apart from the competition and positions you as a leader in the real estate wholesaling coaching industry.

## Online Marketing Techniques

In today's digital era, online marketing has become a crucial aspect of any successful business, including real estate wholesaling. As a beginning real estate investor looking to excel in the competitive market, understanding and implementing effective online marketing techniques can significantly boost your chances of success. This subchapter will provide an in-depth look at some key online marketing strategies specifically tailored to the niche of real estate wholesaling coaching.

# The Beginner's Blueprint to Wholesaling Real Estate: Step-by-Step Coaching for Success

1. Website Optimization: A user-friendly and search engine optimized website is the foundation of any online marketing campaign. Learn the basics of website design and ensure your site is mobile-friendly, loads quickly, and provides relevant information to potential clients.

2. Search Engine Optimization (SEO): SEO techniques help your website rank higher in search engine results, increasing its visibility to potential clients. Research and incorporate relevant keywords, optimize meta tags, and create high-quality content to improve your website's organic search rankings.

3. Pay-Per-Click (PPC) Advertising: PPC advertising allows you to display targeted ads on search engines and social media platforms, reaching potential clients actively searching for real estate investment opportunities. Familiarize yourself with platforms such as Google Ads and Facebook Ads to create compelling campaigns within your budget.

4. Content Marketing: Creating valuable and informative content not only establishes you as an industry expert but also attracts potential clients. Share your knowledge through blog posts, videos, podcasts, and downloadable resources, and promote them through social media channels and email marketing campaigns.

5. Social Media Marketing: Leverage the power of social media platforms to engage with your target audience. Create business profiles on platforms like Facebook, Instagram, LinkedIn, and Twitter, and regularly post relevant content, share success stories, and engage with followers to build brand awareness and credibility.

6. Email Marketing: Build an email list of potential clients and regularly send them newsletters, market updates, and exclusive deals. Craft compelling subject lines and content to increase open rates and conversions.

7. Online Directories and Listings: Register your business on popular online directories and real estate websites to increase your online presence and visibility. Optimize your listings with accurate information, high-quality images, and compelling descriptions.

Remember, consistency and measurement are key to online marketing success. Continuously monitor and analyze your marketing efforts using tools like Google Analytics to identify what works and refine your strategies accordingly. By implementing these online marketing techniques, you will position yourself as a knowledgeable real estate wholesaling coach and attract a steady stream of potential clients, setting yourself up for success in the competitive real estate market.

# Direct Mail Campaigns

# The Beginner's Blueprint to Wholesaling Real Estate: Step-by-Step Coaching for Success

One of the most effective marketing strategies for beginning real estate investors in the niche of real estate wholesaling coaching is direct mail campaigns. Direct mail campaigns involve sending targeted mailings to potential sellers, with the goal of generating leads and ultimately closing deals.

There are several reasons why direct mail campaigns are a powerful tool for real estate investors. Firstly, they allow investors to reach a large number of potential sellers in a cost-effective manner. Unlike other marketing methods that require a significant budget, direct mail campaigns can be tailored to fit any budget, making them accessible to beginning investors.

Secondly, direct mail campaigns offer a personalized approach to reaching potential sellers. By sending physical mailings, investors can stand out from the competition who may solely rely on digital marketing methods. A personalized letter or postcard can create a stronger connection with potential sellers and increase the chances of receiving a response.

When planning a direct mail campaign, it is crucial to define your target audience. This can be done by conducting thorough market research and identifying specific demographics and neighborhoods that align with your investment goals. By narrowing down your target audience, you can create highly targeted mailings that are more likely to resonate with potential sellers.

Crafting compelling and persuasive content for your direct mail pieces is another key aspect of a successful campaign. Your message should be concise, engaging, and highlight the benefits of working with you as a real estate wholesaling coach. Including testimonials or success stories from previous clients can also help build credibility and trust.

Tracking and measuring the results of your direct mail campaign is essential to determine its effectiveness. This can be done by using unique phone numbers or website URLs in your mailings, allowing you to track the number of leads or conversions generated. By analyzing the data, you can make necessary adjustments to improve future campaigns.

In conclusion, direct mail campaigns are a valuable tool for beginning real estate investors in the niche of real estate wholesaling coaching. They offer a cost-effective and personalized approach to reach potential sellers, allowing investors to generate leads and close deals. By defining your target audience, crafting compelling content, and tracking the results, you can create successful direct mail campaigns that drive your real estate wholesaling business forward.

## Bandit Signs and Billboards

When it comes to marketing your real estate wholesaling business, bandit signs and billboards can be powerful tools to reach potential sellers and buyers. In this subchapter, we will explore how these marketing strategies can help you generate leads and increase your chances of success as a beginning real estate investor.

Bandit signs are small, inexpensive signs typically made of corrugated plastic that you can place in high-traffic areas to attract attention. These signs often have a catchy headline and a call-to-action, such as "Sell Your House Fast!" or "We Buy Houses for Cash." They are usually placed on telephone poles, street corners, or in neighborhoods where you want to target motivated sellers. Bandit signs work by grabbing the attention of people who may be looking to sell their properties quickly, and they provide them with an easy way to contact you.

Billboards, on the other hand, are larger and more expensive than bandit signs but can have a greater impact in terms of visibility and brand recognition. Billboards are typically placed along highways or busy streets and can reach a larger audience. They allow you to showcase your brand, message, and contact information to potential sellers and buyers who may be interested in real estate deals. While billboards require a larger investment, they can be worth it if you have a solid marketing budget and want to establish yourself as a serious player in the real estate wholesaling industry.

When using bandit signs and billboards, it is essential to comply with local regulations and obtain any necessary permits. Some cities or municipalities have restrictions on where and how you can place signs or billboards, so make sure to do your research before starting your marketing campaign.

Additionally, track the performance of your bandit signs and billboards to determine their effectiveness. Use unique phone numbers or website URLs on each sign or billboard to track the number of leads generated. This will help you evaluate which locations or designs are working best and optimize your marketing efforts accordingly.

In conclusion, bandit signs and billboards can be valuable marketing tools for beginning real estate investors in the niche of real estate wholesaling coaching. They can help you attract motivated sellers and buyers, increase brand visibility, and establish yourself as a serious player in the industry. However, it is crucial to comply with local regulations and track the performance of your marketing campaigns to ensure maximum effectiveness.

## Utilizing Social Media Platforms

In today's digital age, social media has become an integral part of our lives, and it has also revolutionized the way businesses operate. As a beginning real estate investor, understanding how to leverage social media platforms can be a game-changer for your wholesaling business. In this subchapter, we will explore the various ways you can utilize social media to enhance your real estate wholesaling coaching journey and achieve success.

1. Building an Online Presence: Social media platforms such as Facebook, Instagram, LinkedIn, and Twitter provide you with an opportunity to establish your brand and create an online presence. By consistently posting informative and engaging content related to real estate wholesaling, you can attract a following of potential clients and investors. This will help you build credibility and establish yourself as an authority in the niche.

2. Networking and Relationship Building: Social media platforms offer a unique opportunity to connect with other professionals in the real estate industry. Join relevant groups and communities, participate in discussions, share insights, and network with potential partners, mentors, and investors. Engaging with like-minded individuals can lead to valuable connections and collaborations that can accelerate your success in wholesaling.

3. Targeted Advertising: Social media platforms provide advanced targeting options, allowing you to reach a specific audience for your real estate wholesaling coaching services. Utilize the targeting features to narrow down your audience based on factors such as location, age, income, and interests. By creating compelling ads that resonate with your target audience, you can generate leads and attract potential clients or students.

4. Content Marketing: Social media is an excellent platform for sharing valuable content related to real estate wholesaling. Create informative blog posts, videos, infographics, and podcasts that address common pain points and provide solutions to your target audience. By consistently delivering high-quality content, you can establish yourself as a trusted resource and attract potential clients or students.

5. Engagement and Feedback: Social media platforms allow for real-time engagement with your audience. Respond promptly to comments, messages, and inquiries, as this demonstrates your commitment and professionalism. Encourage feedback from your followers and clients, and use it to improve your wholesaling coaching services.

Remember, social media is a tool, and like any tool, it requires consistent effort and a strategic approach to yield results. By utilizing social media platforms effectively, you can expand your network, attract potential clients, and establish yourself as a reputable wholesaling real estate coach. Embrace the power of social media and watch your real estate wholesaling coaching journey thrive.

# Chapter 7: Financing your Wholesaling Deals

## Funding Options for Wholesalers

As a beginning real estate investor looking to venture into the world of wholesaling, it's important to understand the various funding options available to you. Wholesaling real estate involves finding discounted properties and quickly assigning the contract to another buyer for a profit, without the need for extensive renovations or repairs. However, to successfully execute these deals, you may require access to funds. In this subchapter, we will explore some funding options that can help you kick-start your wholesaling journey.

1. Personal Savings: One of the simplest and most accessible funding options for wholesalers is utilizing personal savings. If you have some money set aside, you can use it as a starting point for your wholesaling business. While this may not be a long-term solution, it can help you get started and build momentum.

2. Private Money Lenders: Private money lenders are individuals or companies that provide loans specifically for real estate investments. They often offer more flexible terms compared to traditional lenders, making them an attractive option for wholesalers. Building relationships with private money lenders can provide you with a consistent source of funding for your deals.

3. Hard Money Lenders: Hard money lenders are similar to private money lenders, but they typically focus on short-term loans for real estate investments. These loans are secured by the property itself, so your credit score or personal financial situation may be less of a factor. Hard money lenders can be a valuable resource, especially if you're dealing with distressed properties.

4. Joint Ventures: Partnering with other real estate investors or wholesalers can be a great way to pool resources and access funding. By combining your expertise and capital, you can tackle larger deals and increase your earning potential. Joint ventures can also provide opportunities for learning and mentorship, which are invaluable for beginning real estate investors.

5. Seller Financing: In some cases, motivated sellers may be willing to offer financing options. This means they will act as the lender and allow you to make payments over time, instead of requiring an upfront cash payment. Seller financing can be an excellent solution when traditional funding sources are limited.

When it comes to funding options for wholesalers, there is no one-size-fits-all solution. It's essential to evaluate each option based on your specific circumstances and goals. By understanding the various funding options available and utilizing them strategically, you can ensure a solid financial foundation for your wholesaling business. Remember, building relationships with lenders and investors is crucial for long-term success in real estate wholesaling.

# Private Lenders and Hard Money Loans

As a beginning real estate investor, one of the key factors that can contribute to your success in real estate wholesaling is the ability to secure funding for your deals. While traditional banks and financial institutions may be hesitant to lend to new investors without an established track record, private lenders and hard money loans present viable alternatives that can help you jumpstart your real estate wholesaling career.

Private lenders are individuals or small groups of investors who are willing to lend their own money for real estate deals. They can be friends, family members, or other investors who are interested in earning a return on their investment. Private lenders are often more flexible and open to working with beginning investors, as they are not bound by the strict regulations and requirements that traditional lenders have.

One of the advantages of working with private lenders is that the loan approval process is typically faster and more straightforward compared to traditional lenders. Private lenders are primarily interested in the potential profitability of the deal and the borrower's ability to repay the loan, rather than focusing on credit scores or financial history. This makes it easier for beginning real estate investors to access the funds they need to close their wholesale deals.

Hard money loans, on the other hand, are specialized loans that are specifically designed for real estate investors. These loans are typically provided by private lenders or companies that specialize in lending to real estate investors. Hard money loans are secured by the property itself, rather than the borrower's creditworthiness, making them an attractive option for beginning investors.

Hard money loans usually have higher interest rates and shorter repayment terms compared to traditional loans. However, they can be an excellent tool for financing your real estate wholesaling deals, especially when you need quick access to funds or when traditional lenders are not an option.

When working with private lenders or considering hard money loans, it's important to do your due diligence and research the terms and conditions of the loan. Make sure you understand the interest rates, repayment terms, and any potential fees or penalties associated with the loan. Building a strong relationship with your private lenders is also crucial, as they can become valuable partners who support your real estate wholesaling endeavors.

In conclusion, private lenders and hard money loans can be valuable resources for beginning real estate investors looking to fund their wholesale deals. By exploring these alternative financing options, you can increase your chances of success and accelerate your progress in the world of real estate wholesaling.

## Creative Financing Strategies

One of the most important aspects of being a successful real estate wholesaler is having access to creative financing strategies. These strategies can help you secure deals and close transactions even when traditional financing options are not available. In this subchapter, we will explore some of the most effective creative financing strategies that beginner real estate investors can use to achieve success in the world of wholesaling.

1. Seller Financing: Seller financing is a powerful tool that allows investors to purchase properties directly from the seller with a loan provided by the seller. This strategy can be particularly useful when dealing with motivated sellers who are open to alternative financing options.

2. Private Money Lenders: Private money lenders are individuals or companies that are willing to lend money for real estate investments. By building relationships with private money lenders, you can access funds that can be used for wholesaling deals, even if you don't have a strong credit history or a large down payment.

3. Hard Money Loans: Hard money loans are short-term, high-interest loans that are typically provided by private investors or companies. While the interest rates may be higher, they offer quick access to funds without the strict requirements of traditional lenders.

4. Subject-To Financing: Subject-to financing involves taking over the existing mortgage of the seller while leaving the loan in their name. This strategy allows you to acquire properties without having to obtain new financing, making it an excellent option for investors with limited funds or credit.

5. Lease Options: Lease options give investors the right to lease a property with the option to buy it at a predetermined price and time frame. This strategy allows you to control a property without having to obtain a mortgage, making it ideal for beginners in real estate wholesaling.

6. Joint Ventures: Joint ventures involve partnering with other investors or individuals to fund a real estate deal. By pooling resources and expertise, you can access larger deals and share the risks and rewards with your partner.

These creative financing strategies are just a few examples of the tools available to beginner real estate investors in the field of wholesaling. By understanding and implementing these strategies, you can significantly increase your chances of success and profitability in the real estate market. Remember, creativity and resourcefulness are key when it comes to finding and securing financing for your wholesaling deals.

## Evaluating Financing Terms

As a beginning real estate investor, understanding and evaluating financing terms is crucial to your success in the world of real estate wholesaling. Financing plays a significant role in any investment, and it's essential to have a firm grasp of the various terms and options available to you.

When evaluating financing terms, there are several key factors to consider. The first is interest rates. Interest rates can greatly impact the overall cost of borrowing and can vary depending on the type of financing you choose. It's important to compare interest rates from different lenders to ensure you secure the best possible rate for your investment.

Another crucial aspect to evaluate is the repayment terms. This includes the length of the loan and the frequency of payments. Longer loan terms may result in lower monthly payments but can also mean paying more in interest over time. Conversely, shorter loan terms may have higher monthly payments but can save you money on interest in the long run. Understanding your cash flow and financial goals will help you determine the most suitable repayment terms for your investment.

Additionally, it's important to consider any associated fees or charges. Lenders often charge origination fees, appraisal fees, and closing costs, among others. These fees can vary significantly between lenders, so it's essential to compare and negotiate these costs to minimize your overall expenses.

Furthermore, it's essential to evaluate the flexibility of the financing terms. Will you have the option to prepay the loan without penalties? Can you refinance the loan if needed? Understanding the flexibility of the financing terms can give you peace of mind and allow you to adapt to changing circumstances.

Lastly, it's crucial to consider the overall financial health of the lender. Working with a reputable and established lender is vital to ensure a smooth and reliable financing process. Research the lender's track record, read reviews, and seek recommendations from other investors to ensure you're partnering with a trustworthy institution.

Evaluating financing terms can be overwhelming, especially for beginning real estate investors. However, by considering factors such as interest rates, repayment terms, fees, flexibility, and the lender's financial health, you can make informed decisions that align with your investment goals. Remember, thorough evaluation is key to securing the best financing terms for your real estate wholesaling ventures.

## Managing Financial Risks

Managing Financial Risks in Real Estate Wholesaling

As a beginning real estate investor venturing into the world of real estate wholesaling, it is crucial to understand and effectively manage the various financial risks associated with this lucrative investment strategy. By implementing sound risk management practices, you can safeguard your investments and pave the way for long-term success in the real estate wholesaling industry.

One of the primary financial risks in real estate wholesaling is the lack of available capital. Wholesaling typically involves quickly finding and assigning contracts to other investors without actually purchasing the property. However, in some cases, you may need to secure the property with earnest money or make other upfront payments. It is essential to have sufficient funds or access to financing options to cover these costs.

To mitigate this risk, building a strong network of investors who can provide financial backing or partnering with a reliable funding source can be advantageous. Additionally, having a solid understanding of your financial limits and setting strict investment criteria will help prevent overextending yourself and reduce the chances of encountering financial difficulties.

Another financial risk in real estate wholesaling is market volatility. Real estate markets can fluctuate, impacting property values and demand. It is crucial to stay updated with market trends and conduct thorough market research before entering into any deals. This will enable you to identify potential risks and make informed decisions to minimize losses.

To manage market volatility, diversifying your investment portfolio is key. By spreading your investments across different markets or property types, you can reduce the impact of market fluctuations on your overall returns. Additionally, establishing contingency plans and exit strategies in case of unfavorable market conditions will help you navigate through challenging times and protect your financial interests.

Lastly, legal and contractual risks must be managed effectively to safeguard your investments. Understanding and complying with local laws and regulations is crucial to avoid costly legal disputes. It is recommended to consult with legal professionals specializing in real estate to ensure that your contracts and agreements are legally sound and protect your interests.

In conclusion, managing financial risks in real estate wholesaling is essential for beginning real estate investors. By establishing a strong financial foundation, staying informed about market trends, and adhering to legal requirements, you can minimize risks and maximize your chances of success. Remember, proper risk management is a continuous process, and continuously educating yourself and adapting your strategies will help you thrive in the real estate wholesaling industry.

# Chapter 8: Scaling Your Wholesaling Business

## Hiring and Building a Team

As a beginning real estate investor venturing into the world of real estate wholesaling, one of the most important aspects of your success is hiring and building a competent team. While it may seem daunting at first, assembling a team of professionals who can support and guide you along your journey is crucial for your long-term success.

One of the first members you should consider adding to your team is a real estate wholesaling coach. A coach can provide you with step-by-step guidance and support, helping you navigate the intricacies of wholesaling real estate. They can teach you the ins and outs of finding motivated sellers, negotiating deals, and closing transactions. A coach can also provide valuable feedback and help you avoid common pitfalls that beginners often fall into.

Another crucial team member is a real estate attorney. Having a trusted attorney on your side is essential to ensure that all legal aspects of your wholesale transactions are properly handled. They can review contracts, assist with title searches, and navigate any legal issues that may arise during the process. Your attorney can also help you understand the laws and regulations specific to your area, ensuring that you stay in compliance and avoid any potential legal troubles.

A reliable and knowledgeable real estate agent is also an asset to your team. They can help you find potential properties, evaluate their market value, and provide you with access to the Multiple Listing Service (MLS). Additionally, a real estate agent can assist you in marketing your wholesale deals to potential buyers, increasing your chances of a successful transaction.

Beyond these core team members, you may also consider adding other professionals such as a reputable contractor, a property inspector, and a mortgage broker. These individuals can help you assess the condition of properties, estimate repair costs, and secure financing for your buyers.

Remember, building a successful real estate wholesaling business is not a one-person endeavor. By assembling a competent team, you can leverage the expertise of others to streamline your operation and increase your chances of success. Continuously seek out individuals who align with your goals and share your passion for real estate wholesaling, as they will be crucial in helping you achieve your financial objectives.

## Automating Wholesaling Processes

In the fast-paced world of real estate wholesaling, time is of the essence. As a beginning real estate investor, you may find yourself overwhelmed by the numerous tasks involved in wholesaling properties. However, with the advent of technology and automation, you can streamline your wholesaling processes, saving time and energy while maximizing your profits.

This subchapter explores the various ways you can automate your wholesaling business and provides step-by-step guidance on implementing these strategies. By embracing automation, you can focus on what matters most – finding and closing deals – while the technology takes care of the rest.

One of the most crucial aspects of wholesaling is lead generation. Without a consistent flow of leads, your business will suffer. In this subchapter, you will learn how to leverage automated marketing tools to generate a steady stream of motivated seller leads. From setting up email marketing campaigns to utilizing social media advertising, you'll discover the power of automation in capturing and nurturing leads.

Once you have leads coming in, it's essential to automate your lead management process. We will guide you through the process of implementing a customer relationship management (CRM) system that will help you organize and track your leads efficiently. You'll learn how to automate follow-ups, schedule appointments, and monitor your pipeline, ensuring no lead falls through the cracks.

In addition to lead generation and management, this subchapter also delves into automating the contract and closing processes. We will introduce you to electronic signature platforms that allow you to send and sign contracts digitally, eliminating the need for physical paperwork and speeding up the closing process.

Furthermore, we will explore virtual wholesaling, a strategy that enables you to conduct your business remotely. By leveraging technology and automation, you can wholesale properties in different markets without ever stepping foot in the area. We will walk you through the tools and techniques necessary for successful virtual wholesaling.

Automating wholesaling processes is not only about efficiency but also scalability. By implementing automation strategies early on in your wholesaling journey, you will be able to handle a larger volume of deals and expand your business in a sustainable manner.

In conclusion, this subchapter provides beginning real estate investors with a comprehensive guide to automating wholesaling processes. From lead generation to contract management, you will learn how to harness the power of technology and automation to streamline your operations, save time, and maximize your success in the world of real estate wholesaling.

## Streamlining Deal Management

As a beginning real estate investor, one of the most crucial skills you need to develop is efficient deal management. Real estate wholesaling, in particular, requires a well-organized and streamlined approach to ensure success. In this subchapter, we will explore the key strategies and techniques that will help you streamline your deal management process and maximize your chances of success in the competitive world of real estate wholesaling.

1. Establishing a System: To streamline your deal management, it's essential to establish a systematic process from start to finish. This includes setting up a dedicated workspace, creating a filing system for documents, and utilizing technology tools such as customer relationship management (CRM) software to track leads, contacts, and deals.

2. Lead Generation and Qualification: Efficient deal management begins with effective lead generation and qualification. Learn various marketing strategies to attract motivated sellers and pre-screen them to determine if they meet your investment criteria. This will ensure that you focus your time and energy on the most promising leads, increasing your chances of closing deals.

3. Deal Analysis and Negotiation: Streamlining your deal management process involves conducting swift and accurate deal analysis. Develop a standardized checklist to evaluate potential properties, considering key factors such as location, condition, potential repairs, and market value. Additionally, hone your negotiation skills to secure the best possible price and terms for your wholesale deals.

4. Documentation and Contracts: To streamline deal management, it is essential to have a clear understanding of the necessary documentation and contracts involved in real estate wholesaling. Familiarize yourself with purchase agreements, assignment contracts, and other legal documents required to protect your interests and ensure a smooth transaction.

5. Team Building and Outsourcing: As your real estate wholesaling business grows, it becomes crucial to build a reliable team and outsource certain tasks. This could include hiring virtual assistants, property inspectors, contractors, or real estate attorneys. Delegating responsibilities will allow you to focus on deal sourcing, analysis, and negotiation, further streamlining your deal management process.

6. Analytics and Reporting: Lastly, leveraging data analytics and reporting tools will help you monitor and evaluate the success of your deal management efforts. By tracking key performance metrics such as conversion rates, average profit per deal, and marketing expenses, you can identify areas for improvement and make data-driven decisions to optimize your wholesaling business.

Remember, streamlining your deal management process requires ongoing learning, adaptation, and refinement. By implementing these strategies and techniques, you will gain a competitive edge in the world of real estate wholesaling coaching and increase your chances of success as a beginning real estate investor.

# Expanding into New Markets

As a beginning real estate investor, one of the most important steps you can take to grow your business is expanding into new markets. Exploring new territories will not only provide you with a wider range of opportunities but also increase your chances of success in the competitive world of real estate wholesaling. In this subchapter, we will discuss the strategies and considerations for expanding into new markets, ensuring that you have a solid blueprint for success.

The first step in expanding into new markets is conducting thorough market research. Understanding the local dynamics, such as supply and demand, market trends, and economic factors, is crucial for making informed decisions. Analyzing data from multiple sources, such as local real estate associations, government reports, and online platforms, will give you a comprehensive understanding of the new market's potential.

Once you have identified a promising market, it's essential to build a strong network of local contacts. This includes real estate agents, property inspectors, appraisers, and other professionals who can provide valuable insights and support. Attending local real estate networking events, joining investor groups, and utilizing online platforms can help you connect with the right people and build relationships that will be instrumental in your success.

Expanding into new markets also requires adapting your marketing strategies. Each market has its own unique characteristics and target audience, so it's crucial to tailor your marketing efforts accordingly. This could include adjusting your messaging, targeting specific neighborhoods or demographics, and utilizing local advertising channels. A well-crafted marketing plan will ensure that your message reaches the right people and generates leads in the new market.

Furthermore, expanding into new markets may require adjusting your operational processes. This includes understanding local regulations, licensing requirements, and legal considerations. Working with local attorneys and consultants can help you navigate these complexities and ensure compliance with local laws.

Finally, it's important to continuously evaluate and reassess your expansion efforts. Regularly review your performance in the new market, track key metrics, and make adjustments as necessary. This iterative approach will allow you to optimize your strategies and maximize your success.

In conclusion, expanding into new markets is a crucial step for beginning real estate investors looking to excel in the realm of wholesaling. By conducting thorough market research, building a strong network, adapting marketing strategies, and adjusting operational processes, you can position yourself for success in new territories. Remember, expanding into new markets is not without its challenges, but with the right blueprint and dedication, you can achieve substantial growth and create a thriving wholesaling business.

## Setting Long-term Goals for Growth

As a beginning real estate investor, it is essential to have a clear vision of your long-term goals for growth. In the world of real estate wholesaling, where success is built on strategic planning and consistent efforts, setting goals becomes even more critical. This subchapter will guide you through the process of establishing long-term goals that will propel your real estate wholesaling career forward.

The first step in setting long-term goals is to have a clear understanding of what you want to achieve. Take some time to envision where you see yourself in five or ten years. Do you want to build a thriving real estate wholesaling business? Are you looking to expand into other areas of real estate investing? Whatever your aspirations may be, write them down and make them tangible.

Once you have a clear vision, break it down into smaller, manageable goals. These short-term goals will serve as stepping stones towards your long-term objectives. For example, if you aim to close ten deals within the next year, set smaller goals such as acquiring a certain number of leads each month or attending networking events regularly. By breaking down your long-term goals, you can track your progress and stay motivated along the way.

Additionally, setting specific, measurable, attainable, relevant, and time-bound (SMART) goals is crucial. This framework ensures that your goals are well-defined and actionable. For instance, instead of setting a vague goal like "increase revenue," set a SMART goal like "increase revenue by 20% within the next six months by closing three additional deals per month."

Moreover, it is crucial to regularly review and adjust your goals as you progress in your real estate wholesaling journey. As you gain experience and expertise, your goals may evolve or change entirely. Be open to adapting your goals to align with your growing knowledge and aspirations.

Lastly, seek out real estate wholesaling coaching to accelerate your growth and ensure you stay on track. A reputable coach can provide guidance, accountability, and valuable insights into the industry. They can help you refine your goals and develop a personalized roadmap for success.

In conclusion, setting long-term goals for growth is an essential aspect of real estate wholesaling. By having a clear vision, breaking it down into smaller goals, and utilizing the SMART framework, you can create a roadmap to success. Regularly reviewing and adjusting your goals, as well as seeking guidance from a real estate wholesaling coach, will further enhance your chances of achieving your long-term objectives. Remember, success in real estate wholesaling is a journey, and setting meaningful goals will help you stay focused, motivated, and ultimately reach your full potential.

# Chapter 9: Overcoming Challenges and Pitfalls

## Dealing with Rejections and Failures

Failure and rejection are inevitable parts of any journey, especially in the world of real estate wholesaling. As a beginning real estate investor, it is crucial to understand that setbacks are a normal part of the process. Learning how to handle rejections and failures will not only help you navigate through the challenges but also set you up for success in the long run.

One of the first things to remember when facing rejection is to avoid taking it personally. Rejections are not a reflection of your worth or abilities; instead, they are simply a part of the learning curve. Real estate wholesaling requires resilience and persistence, and every rejection brings you one step closer to a successful deal. Embrace the rejection as an opportunity to grow and improve your skills.

Another important aspect of dealing with failures is to analyze the situation objectively. Take a step back and evaluate what went wrong. Did you make any mistakes in your approach? Did you miss any crucial details? By identifying the areas where you can improve, you can turn your failures into valuable lessons. Remember, failure is not the end; it is an opportunity for growth.

Building a support system is also essential for handling rejections and failures. Surround yourself with like-minded individuals who have gone through similar experiences. Join real estate wholesaling coaching programs or connect with mentors who can provide guidance and support. Sharing your struggles with others who have been there can provide valuable insights and help you stay motivated during tough times.

Moreover, it is crucial to maintain a positive mindset. Real estate wholesaling can be a roller coaster ride, with highs and lows. When faced with failures, it is easy to lose motivation and give up. However, a positive mindset will help you stay focused on your goals and push through the obstacles. Celebrate every small victory and remind yourself of the progress you have made so far.

Lastly, learn from successful investors who have overcome failures and achieved their goals. Reading books, attending seminars, or listening to podcasts can provide you with valuable insights and strategies for dealing with rejections and failures. By learning from those who have walked the path before you, you can avoid common pitfalls and increase your chances of success.

Remember, failure and rejection are not signs of defeat but stepping stones towards success. Embrace them, learn from them, and let them fuel your determination to become a successful real estate wholesaler. With the right mindset, support system, and continuous learning, you can overcome any obstacle and achieve your goals in the world of real estate wholesaling.

## Managing Time and Priorities

As a beginning real estate investor, one of the most important skills you can develop is effective time management and prioritization. In the fast-paced world of real estate wholesaling, where deals can come and go in the blink of an eye, it is crucial to have a system in place to ensure that you are making the most out of every minute of your day. This subchapter will provide you with practical strategies and techniques to help you manage your time and priorities effectively, ultimately leading to your success in the real estate wholesaling industry.

The first step in managing your time and priorities is to establish clear goals. What do you want to achieve as a real estate wholesaler? Setting specific, measurable, achievable, relevant, and time-bound (SMART) goals will provide you with a roadmap to follow and enable you to prioritize your tasks effectively. By knowing what you want to accomplish, you can focus on the most important activities that will bring you closer to your goals.

Next, it is essential to create a schedule or a daily routine. Allocate dedicated time slots for prospecting, lead generation, networking, analyzing deals, and other crucial activities. By structuring your day, you can avoid wasting time on unproductive tasks and ensure that you are consistently working towards your goals.

To enhance your time management skills, consider using productivity tools and techniques. Utilize technology to your advantage by leveraging project management software, task management apps, and calendar tools to keep your tasks organized and deadlines on track. Additionally, practice techniques such as the Pomodoro Technique, where you work in focused bursts of time followed by short breaks, to increase your productivity and avoid burnout.

Another crucial aspect of managing time and priorities is learning to delegate and outsource tasks. As a beginning real estate investor, you may find yourself wearing multiple hats and handling various responsibilities. However, it is important to recognize when certain tasks can be delegated or outsourced to others, allowing you to focus on higher-value activities. Whether it is hiring an assistant, a virtual assistant, or partnering with professionals in the industry, delegating tasks can free up your time to concentrate on growing your business.

Lastly, remember to prioritize self-care. Real estate wholesaling can be demanding and stressful, but taking care of yourself is vital for long-term success. Make time for exercise, relaxation, and hobbies to recharge and maintain a healthy work-life balance. By managing your time effectively and prioritizing self-care, you can ensure that you have the energy and focus necessary to excel in the real estate wholesaling industry.

In conclusion, managing time and priorities is essential for beginning real estate investors in the niche of real estate wholesaling coaching. By setting clear goals, creating a schedule, utilizing productivity tools, delegating tasks, and prioritizing self-care, you can maximize your effectiveness, increase productivity, and achieve success in the real estate wholesaling industry.

## Handling Legal Issues

As a beginning real estate investor, one of the most crucial aspects of your business is understanding and effectively handling legal issues. In the world of real estate wholesaling, where deals are made quickly and profits can be substantial, it is essential to have a solid understanding of the legal framework that governs this industry. This subchapter will provide you with a comprehensive overview of the legal issues you may encounter as a real estate wholesaler and equip you with the tools and knowledge necessary to navigate them successfully.

One of the primary legal considerations in real estate wholesaling is ensuring compliance with local, state, and federal laws. Each jurisdiction has its own set of regulations and requirements that must be followed, ranging from licensing and registration to disclosure and marketing restrictions. Understanding these laws and staying updated on any changes is crucial to avoid legal complications and potential financial penalties.

Another important legal aspect to consider is contracts. As a wholesaler, you will be involved in negotiating and assigning contracts between sellers and buyers. It is vital to have a thorough understanding of contract law and to use legally binding agreements that protect your interests and clearly outline the terms of the transaction. This subchapter will provide you with examples of effective contract templates that you can use to streamline your business operations.

Additionally, it is essential to have a grasp of fair housing laws and regulations. Discrimination in real estate transactions based on factors such as race, color, religion, sex, or national origin is strictly prohibited. Familiarize yourself with fair housing laws to ensure that you conduct your business ethically and avoid any legal repercussions.

Finally, this subchapter will delve into the importance of working with legal professionals. Building a network of reliable attorneys who specialize in real estate transactions is crucial to your success as a wholesaler. They can provide guidance, review contracts, and offer advice on complex legal matters that you may encounter throughout your journey.

Remember, in the world of real estate wholesaling, ignorance of the law is not an excuse. By dedicating time and effort to understanding and handling legal issues, you will protect yourself, your business, and your reputation as a beginning real estate investor. With the knowledge gained from this subchapter, you will be equipped to navigate the legal landscape confidently and successfully as you embark on your real estate wholesaling journey.

## Coping with Market Fluctuations

As a beginning real estate investor, one of the key challenges you will face is coping with market fluctuations. The real estate market is known for its ups and downs, and being able to navigate through these fluctuations is crucial for your success as a wholesaler. In this subchapter, we will explore some effective strategies and techniques to help you cope with market fluctuations and thrive in any market condition.

1. Stay Informed: The first step in coping with market fluctuations is to stay informed about the latest trends and developments in the real estate market. Keep a close eye on market indicators such as housing inventory, interest rates, and local economic conditions. By understanding the current state of the market, you can make informed decisions and adjust your strategies accordingly.

2. Diversify Your Portfolio: Another effective way to cope with market fluctuations is to diversify your real estate portfolio. Don't put all your eggs in one basket. Instead, consider investing in different types of properties, in different locations. This will help to minimize your risk and provide you with a buffer against any market downturns.

3. Adapt Your Strategies: In a volatile market, it's essential to be flexible and adapt your strategies as needed. For example, if the market is experiencing a slowdown, you may need to adjust your pricing or marketing strategies to attract buyers. Stay open-minded and be willing to try new approaches to stay ahead of the competition.

4. Build Relationships: Building strong relationships with other real estate professionals is crucial in coping with market fluctuations. Network with local real estate agents, investors, and wholesalers who have experience in different market conditions. By leveraging their expertise and knowledge, you can gain valuable insights and learn from their experiences.

5. Focus on Cash Flow: In uncertain market conditions, it's important to focus on cash flow. Look for properties that can generate positive cash flow, even in a down market. This will provide you with a steady income stream and help you weather any market fluctuations.

Remember, coping with market fluctuations is a continuous process. The real estate market is dynamic, and being able to adapt and adjust your strategies is essential for long-term success. By staying informed, diversifying your portfolio, adapting your strategies, building relationships, and focusing on cash flow, you will be well-equipped to navigate through any market condition and achieve success as a real estate wholesaler.

## Staying Motivated and Focused

# The Beginner's Blueprint to Wholesaling Real Estate: Step-by-Step Coaching for Success

In the fast-paced world of real estate wholesaling, staying motivated and focused is the key to success. As a beginning real estate investor, you need to develop a strong mindset that will help you overcome challenges and achieve your goals. This subchapter will provide you with valuable tips and techniques to stay motivated and focused throughout your wholesaling journey.

One of the first steps in staying motivated is to define your goals. Take the time to write down your short-term and long-term goals. This will give you a clear direction and a sense of purpose. Keep your goals visible and review them regularly to stay focused on what you want to achieve.

Another effective way to stay motivated is to surround yourself with like-minded individuals. Join real estate wholesaling coaching groups or forums where you can connect with other investors who are on the same path as you. Being part of a supportive community will not only keep you motivated but also provide you with valuable insights and advice.

Maintaining a positive mindset is crucial in staying motivated and focused. Real estate wholesaling can be challenging, but it's important to believe in yourself and your abilities. Embrace failure as a learning opportunity and keep pushing forward. Remember, every setback brings you one step closer to success.

To stay focused, it's essential to manage your time effectively. Create a schedule and set aside dedicated time for wholesaling activities. Prioritize your tasks and eliminate distractions that may hinder your progress. By staying organized and disciplined, you'll be able to accomplish more and stay on track.

Rewarding yourself for small achievements can also help you stay motivated. Celebrate each milestone you reach, whether it's closing your first deal or securing a new lead. By recognizing your progress, you'll fuel your motivation to continue working towards your ultimate goals.

Lastly, never underestimate the power of continuous learning. Stay updated on industry trends, attend workshops, and read books on real estate wholesaling. The more knowledge and skills you acquire, the more confident and focused you'll become.

In conclusion, staying motivated and focused is crucial for success in real estate wholesaling. Define your goals, surround yourself with a supportive community, cultivate a positive mindset, manage your time effectively, reward yourself for achievements, and never stop learning. By implementing these strategies, you'll be well on your way to becoming a successful real estate wholesaler.

# Chapter 10: Taking Your Wholesaling Business to the Next Level

## Advanced Wholesaling Strategies

As a beginning real estate investor, you may have already learned the basics of wholesaling real estate and successfully closed a few deals. However, if you truly want to take your wholesaling business to the next level, it's time to explore advanced wholesaling strategies that can maximize your profits and ensure long-term success. In this subchapter, we will delve into some powerful techniques that will help you become a highly successful wholesaler.

One advanced strategy is building a strong network of real estate professionals. By establishing relationships with realtors, appraisers, contractors, and other key players in the industry, you will gain access to valuable resources and information. These connections can help you find hidden deals, negotiate better contracts, and expedite the closing process. Networking is a vital aspect of real estate wholesaling coaching, and with the right network, you can significantly enhance your business.

Another advanced technique is implementing targeted marketing campaigns. While traditional marketing methods like bandit signs and direct mail can still be effective, you need to go beyond these basic strategies to stand out in a competitive market. Utilize digital marketing platforms such as social media, search engine optimization, and email marketing to reach a wider audience. By leveraging technology and analytics, you can target specific demographics and generate high-quality leads that are more likely to convert into profitable deals.

In addition, mastering negotiation skills is crucial for advanced wholesaling success. As you progress in your wholesaling journey, you will encounter more complex deals and challenging sellers. Being able to effectively negotiate terms and prices will give you an edge over your competitors. Study negotiation techniques, learn how to overcome objections, and practice active listening to build rapport with sellers. The ability to negotiate favorable deals is a key skill that all successful wholesalers possess.

Lastly, consider expanding your wholesaling business by exploring new markets or niches. While you may have started wholesaling in a particular area, there could be lucrative opportunities waiting in other locations or property types. Research emerging markets, analyze market trends, and adapt your strategies accordingly. By diversifying your portfolio and staying informed about market shifts, you can stay ahead of the curve and capitalize on untapped opportunities.

In conclusion, advanced wholesaling strategies are essential for beginning real estate investors looking to elevate their wholesaling business. By building a strong network, implementing targeted marketing campaigns, mastering negotiation skills, and exploring new markets, you can maximize your profits and achieve long-term success in the world of real estate wholesaling. Continuously educate yourself, stay flexible, and adapt your strategies to stay ahead of the competition. With dedication and the right guidance, you can become a highly successful wholesaler in no time.

## Partnering with Other Investors

One of the most effective strategies for success in real estate wholesaling is partnering with other investors. Collaboration can bring a wealth of benefits, including increased access to deals, shared resources, and additional expertise. This subchapter will explore the advantages of partnering with other investors and provide practical tips for forming successful partnerships in the world of real estate wholesaling.

Access to Deals: Partnering with other investors can significantly expand your access to deals. By combining your networks and resources, you can tap into a wider range of opportunities. One investor may have connections with motivated sellers, while another may have a deep understanding of a particular market. By pooling your knowledge and resources, you can uncover deals that would be hard to find on your own.

Shared Resources: Partnering with other investors allows you to share the financial burden and resources required for successful wholesaling. You can split the costs of marketing, lead generation, and closing deals, reducing the individual financial risk. Additionally, by working together, you can leverage each other's strengths and skills, creating a more efficient and effective wholesaling operation.

Additional Expertise: Partnering with experienced investors can provide invaluable expertise and mentorship. By teaming up with someone who has been in the industry for longer, you can tap into their knowledge, learn from their mistakes, and accelerate your learning curve. This mentorship can be a game-changer for beginning real estate investors, providing guidance and support as they navigate the complex world of wholesaling.

Tips for Successful Partnerships: When forming partnerships in real estate wholesaling, it is crucial to establish clear expectations and roles from the beginning. Communicate openly and honestly about your goals, strengths, and weaknesses. A well-defined partnership agreement can help prevent misunderstandings and conflicts down the line. Additionally, it is essential to choose partners who share your values and work ethic to ensure a harmonious and productive relationship.

In conclusion, partnering with other investors is a powerful strategy for success in real estate wholesaling. By collaborating with like-minded individuals, you can access more deals, share resources, and gain valuable expertise. However, it is crucial to approach partnerships with clear expectations, open communication, and a shared vision for success. With the right partners by your side, you can accelerate your wholesaling journey and achieve greater results in the competitive real estate market.

## Exploring Additional Real Estate Ventures

As a beginning real estate investor, your journey in the world of real estate wholesaling coaching has just begun. You have learned the basics of finding distressed properties, negotiating with motivated sellers, and assigning contracts for a profit. Now, it's time to expand your horizons and explore additional real estate ventures that can further enhance your success and profitability.

One of the most logical next steps in your real estate journey is to start rehabbing properties. Rehabbing, also known as fix and flip, involves purchasing distressed properties, renovating them, and selling them for a profit. This strategy allows you to tap into a different segment of the market and potentially generate even higher returns. However, it comes with its own set of challenges, such as managing contractors, estimating renovation costs accurately, and dealing with unexpected issues that may arise during the rehab process. By incorporating rehabbing into your real estate ventures, you can diversify your portfolio and increase your potential for long-term success.

Another avenue worth exploring is buy and hold investing. This strategy involves acquiring properties and holding onto them for an extended period, typically renting them out to generate passive income. While it may not offer immediate profits like wholesaling or rehabbing, buy and hold investing provides a steady stream of income and the potential for long-term appreciation. It also allows you to build equity and leverage your assets to acquire more properties over time. Successful buy and hold investors often enjoy the benefits of cash flow, tax advantages, and wealth accumulation through real estate.

Additionally, as you gain experience and confidence in your real estate ventures, you may want to consider branching out into commercial real estate. Commercial properties, such as office buildings, retail spaces, or warehouses, offer different opportunities and often higher profit margins compared to residential properties. However, commercial real estate investing requires a deeper understanding of market dynamics, leasing agreements, and property management. It may be wise to seek further education or mentorship in this niche before diving in.

Exploring additional real estate ventures beyond wholesaling can open up new doors of opportunity for beginning real estate investors. Whether you choose to venture into rehabbing, buy and hold investing, or commercial real estate, remember to continue educating yourself, networking with industry professionals, and staying up-to-date with market trends. With the right knowledge, mindset, and perseverance, you can navigate these new ventures and continue to grow your real estate portfolio with confidence.

# Continual Learning and Education

In the ever-evolving world of real estate wholesaling, knowledge is power. As a beginning real estate investor, it is crucial to understand the importance of continual learning and education in order to achieve success in this competitive industry. This subchapter will delve into why ongoing education is essential, how it can benefit you as a real estate wholesaler, and provide practical strategies to enhance your learning journey.

Why is continual learning necessary for real estate wholesaling? The answer lies in the dynamic nature of the market. Real estate trends, laws, and regulations are constantly changing, and staying updated is crucial to navigate this complex landscape effectively. Additionally, continual learning enables you to acquire new skills and strategies, allowing you to adapt to market shifts and stay ahead of the competition.

So, how can ongoing education benefit you as a real estate wholesaler? Firstly, it provides you with a solid foundation of knowledge. By immersing yourself in real estate education, you will gain a deep understanding of the industry, including concepts such as market analysis, property valuation, and negotiation tactics. This knowledge will empower you to make informed decisions and increase your chances of success.

Continual learning also helps you develop a growth mindset. By constantly seeking new information and expanding your skill set, you become more adaptable and open to change. This mindset is crucial in real estate wholesaling, as it allows you to overcome challenges, seize opportunities, and continually improve your strategies.

To enhance your learning journey, consider implementing the following strategies:

1. Attend real estate wholesaling coaching programs: Seek out experienced mentors and coaches who specialize in real estate wholesaling. Their guidance and expertise can provide invaluable insights and help you avoid common pitfalls.

2. Read books and publications: Immerse yourself in real estate literature. Books written by successful real estate investors can offer practical tips, strategies, and inspiration.

3. Join online communities and forums: Engage with like-minded individuals in online communities and forums. Here, you can share experiences, ask questions, and learn from the experiences of others.

4. Attend workshops and seminars: Take advantage of workshops and seminars conducted by industry experts. These events provide opportunities to network, gain knowledge, and stay updated with the latest trends.

Remember, education is a lifelong journey. As a beginning real estate investor, continually seek opportunities to learn, grow, and adapt. By embracing continual learning, you will equip yourself with the tools necessary to thrive in the dynamic world of real estate wholesaling.

## Creating a Legacy in Real Estate Wholesaling

As a beginning real estate investor, you have chosen an exciting and potentially lucrative path in the world of real estate wholesaling. Wholesaling offers a unique opportunity to generate profits without the need for extensive capital or credit. However, to truly succeed in this niche, it is important to focus not just on short-term gains but also on creating a lasting legacy in real estate wholesaling.

Building a legacy in real estate wholesaling means leaving a positive impact on the industry and setting yourself up for sustained success. It means establishing a reputation as someone who consistently delivers value, builds strong relationships, and operates with integrity. So, how can you start creating your own legacy in real estate wholesaling? Here are some essential steps to consider:

# The Beginner's Blueprint to Wholesaling Real Estate: Step by-Step Coaching for Success

1. Education and Skill Development: To become a respected authority in real estate wholesaling, it is crucial to continuously educate yourself and develop your skillset. Seek out reputable real estate wholesaling coaching programs, attend seminars, join online forums, and read books written by successful wholesalers. The more knowledge and expertise you acquire, the better equipped you will be to navigate the complexities of this industry.

2. Networking and Building Relationships: Wholesaling is a people-centric business, and your success will greatly depend on the quality of your relationships. Attend real estate networking events, join local investor groups, and connect with experienced wholesalers. Building a strong network will not only provide you with valuable insights and opportunities but also help establish your credibility and reputation.

3. Ethical and Transparent Practices: Real estate wholesaling, like any other business, requires ethical behavior and transparent practices. Always be honest with sellers, investors, and all parties involved in your transactions. By maintaining high ethical standards, you will not only build trust and credibility but also attract repeat business and referrals.

4. Delivering Value: Strive to provide exceptional value to both sellers and investors. Develop a reputation for finding lucrative deals and matching them with the right buyers. By consistently delivering results, you will establish yourself as a reliable wholesaler, paving the way for long-term success.

5. Giving Back: As you progress in your real estate wholesaling journey, consider giving back to the community and industry that has supported you. Share your knowledge and experiences through coaching, mentoring, or writing articles and books. By helping others succeed, you contribute to the growth and development of real estate wholesaling as a whole.

Creating a legacy in real estate wholesaling requires dedication, continuous learning, and a commitment to ethical practices. By focusing on long-term success rather than short-term gains, you can establish yourself as a respected authority and leave a lasting impact on the industry. Embrace these principles, and watch your real estate wholesaling career flourish.

# Conclusion: Your Journey to Wholesaling Success Begins Now!

Congratulations on reaching the end of "The Beginner's Blueprint to Wholesaling Real Estate: Step-by-Step Coaching for Success." You have taken the first step towards becoming a successful real estate wholesaler, and your journey starts now!

Throughout this book, we have provided you with a comprehensive guide to wholesaling real estate. We have covered the basics, from understanding what wholesaling is and how it works, to finding motivated sellers, negotiating deals, and closing transactions. We have also shared valuable tips and strategies that will help you navigate the challenges and pitfalls commonly faced by beginning real estate investors.

As a beginning real estate investor, you have chosen an exciting and potentially lucrative niche in the real estate industry. Wholesaling offers a unique opportunity to earn substantial profits with minimal risk and investment. With the right mindset, knowledge, and dedication, you can achieve great success in this field.

Now that you have completed this book, it's time to put your newfound knowledge into action. Take what you have learned and start implementing it immediately. Remember, education without action is merely entertainment. The real transformation happens when you take action and apply what you have learned.

To further enhance your journey to wholesaling success, consider seeking a real estate wholesaling coach or mentor. A coach can provide personalized guidance, support, and accountability, ensuring that you stay on track and make progress towards your goals. Real estate wholesaling coaching programs are designed specifically for beginners like you, helping you avoid common mistakes and accelerate your success.

In addition to coaching, continue to educate yourself by attending real estate investing seminars, webinars, and workshops. Network with other investors, join real estate investment groups, and participate in online forums to connect with like-minded individuals who can share their experiences and offer valuable insights.

Remember, wholesaling real estate is a business, and like any business, it requires hard work, determination, and perseverance. Be prepared to face challenges, setbacks, and rejection along the way. But also remember that every challenge presents an opportunity for growth and learning.

Stay focused on your goals, maintain a positive mindset, and never stop learning and improving. Keep pushing forward, and success will come.

Your journey to wholesaling success begins now. Embrace the learning process, take action, and watch your dreams of financial freedom and success become a reality.

Best of luck on your wholesaling journey!